The Spiritual Writings of Archimandrite Seraphim Aleksiev

Joy of All Who Sorrow Icon of the Mother of God

The Meaning of Suffering

AND

Strife & Reconciliation

VOLUMES II & III OF

THE SPIRITUAL WRITINGS OF
ARCHIMANDRITE SERAPHIM ALEKSIEV

Translated by Ralitsa Doynova

ST. HERMAN BROTHERHOOD
ST. XENIA SKETE
1994

Address all correspondence to:
St. Xenia Skete
40500 Highway 36 West
Wildwood, CA 96076

Front cover: Icon of Saints Peter and Paul from Chios, Greece.

Publishers Cataloging in Publication
Seraphim Aleksiev, Archimandrite
    The meaning of suffering and
    strife and reconciliation
    Translated from the Bulgarian.
Library of Congress Catalogue Number: 94-69053
ISBN: 0-938635-86-7

✌ CONTENTS ✌

Archimandrite Seraphim (Aleksiev)

About the Author

ARCHIMANDRITE SERAPHIM Aleksiev was born in 1912 in Bulgaria. He acquired his education in the Theological Seminary in Sofia, and afterwards went to study in Switzerland. In 1940 he took monastic vows. His acquaintance with Archbishop Seraphim Sobolev (†1950)[1] played a decisive role in his life. In the person of the Archbishop, Archimandrite Seraphim found an irreplaceable guide in the Faith and in his spiritual life.

Three periods can be defined in the life and creative work of Father Seraphim. During the first (1947-1960), he, as the director of the Cultural and Educational Department of the Holy Synod and despite the difficult conditions of the time, maintained tireless pastoral activity, delivered inspired sermons and lectures, and wrote brochures and books on spiritual and

---

1. Editor's Note: Archbishop Seraphim Sobolev not only was an outstanding theologian defending traditional Orthodoxy, but was also not devoid of the mystical experience of the saints. He had a close relationship, through prayer, with St. Seraphim of Sarov, with whose blessing he embraced monasticism. His stand for Orthodox dogmatic purity and precision was especially pivotal through his defense of the holy Cross, when the heresy of stavroclasm (a heretical "Dogma of Redemption" which denies the saving value of the Cross) infiltrated the Orthodox Church in the late 1920's and 30's. Also, his thick volume against the heretical understanding of "Sophia" is imperative for today's English-speaking faithful. The erroneous teaching of "sophiology" is gaining momentum in revived gnosticism based on the theories of S. Bulgakov, theories which "unite" Orthodox Christians with the neo-pagan New Age movement of today.

moral themes and many poems. The collections of lectures *Our Hope* and *Our Love,* two of his most popular books, are very characteristic of this period. During the second period (1960-1969), Archimandrite Seraphim—at this time an Assistant Professor in Dogmatic Theology in the Theological Academy in Sofia—published a series of theological studies. The third period began in 1969, when he was forced to leave the Theological Academy because of a disagreement in principle with the calendar reform, which was adopted then, and with the pro-ecumenical policy in which the Bulgarian Orthodox Church is involved. Outside the Academy, Archimandrite Seraphim wrote a new series of books with a theological, spiritual, and moral content, among which was his last book and legacy: *Orthodoxy and Ecumenism* (1992)—an in-depth criticism of the ecumenical heresy.

Archimandrite Seraphim reposed on January 13/26, 1993. He left us a precious inheritance: his books and his example of zealous monastic life wholly dedicated to the service of the holy Orthodox Faith.

Introduction

*The choir of Saints have found the fountain of life
and the door of Paradise. May I also find the way
through repentance. I am the lost sheep,
call me back, O Savior, and save me.*
From the Panikhida Service

As the author so aptly states in the first chapter of this book: "The question of suffering is one of the most sensitive questions. Many people ask themselves: why has God created us to suffer in the world from different diseases, sorrows, calamities, troubles and misfortunes?... For those who do not believe in God, this world is a hopeless valley of sorrows." According to the Apostle's word, suffering takes on a very different meaning, for *godly sorrow worketh repentance to salvation not to be repented of: but the sorrow of the world worketh death* (II Cor. 7:10). This Gospel truth has been forgotten; the world rushes to psychologists, psychiatrists, hypnotists, the Eastern practices of yoga, meditation, transcendentalism, etc., looking for answers, but to no avail. Archimandrite Seraphim points us back in the right direction and gives the example of the holy Prophet King David, who praised God in his suffering and "found the lost joy of human life in his longing for God.... How much more possible this is after the coming of Jesus Christ, Who came to earth to renew and regenerate fallen human nature, to restore to us grace and the lost paradisiacal bliss."

9

Righteous Abel.
Icon from the Sypanov Trinity Monastery, Russia, 1676.

INTRODUCTION

Along with the current lack of belief and faith in God, truly the most piteous of all suffering today is the lack of repentance—and therefore the lack of love. Repentance leads to the gateway of heaven and not only alleviates the anguish of suffering but actually transforms this suffering into the intense joy of being reunited with our Lord Jesus Christ. "Having torn up the handwriting of our sins, O Christ, by Thy divine grace, renew in us the grace that makes us sons of God, O Word of God, and grant us to please Thee henceforth with the service of our repentance, that with Thy saints we may sing to Thee: Alleluia."[1]

In today's world gone mad with wars, rumors of wars, strife among families and friends, and with no willingness for reconciliation—the television and media so vividly reflecting this with scenes and accounts of violence world-wide—let us, on our knees, humble ourselves under the Almighty hand of God, turning inward to the arena of our own hearts where the true battle lies, and through repentance cleanse ourselves of the filth of sin and bring forth the fruits of the Spirit: *love, joy, peace, longsuffering, gentleness, goodness, faith, meekness, temperance: against such there is no law* (Gal. 5:22-23), that we, too, with the disciple whom Jesus loved may be able to say, *And the Spirit and the bride say, Come. And let him that heareth say, Come. And let him that is athirst come. And whosoever will, let him take the water of life freely.... He which testifieth these things saith, Surely I come quickly. Amen. Even so, come, Lord Jesus* (Rev. 22:17, 20).

St. Xenia Skete
Protection of the Mother of God, 1994

---

1. From the Akathist of Sts. Sergius and Herman of Valaam, Kontakion 12.

The Crucifixion of Our Lord Jesus Christ, Icon from Greece

VOLUME II

The Meaning of Suffering

BY ARCHIMANDRITE SERAPHIM ALEKSIEV

Translated by Ralitsa Doynova

Righteous King David, who in his suffering praised God.

❧ *Part 1* ❧

Suffering in the Light of Divine Revelation

Unconsolable Sorrow, by E. N. Kramskoy, 1884, Russia.

Suffering in the Light of Divine Revelation

My son, despise not the chastening of the Lord;
neither be weary of his correction: for whom the Lord loveth
he chasteneth; and scourgeth every son whom he receiveth.
Proverbs 3:11-12; Hebrews 12:6

THE QUESTION of suffering is one of the most sensitive questions. Many ask themselves: why has God created us to suffer in this world from different diseases, sorrows, calamities, troubles, and misfortunes; from passions on the inside, from bad people on the outside, from the envy of neighbors, from the menace of enemies? For those who do not believe in God, this world is a hopeless valley of sorrows; life for them is a sad symphony of wailing and weeping. Some in their despair even say that there is no other hell beyond the grave, that hell is here, on earth. In this way earthly sorrows, not being lightened by the hopes of heavenly Revelation, lead to pessimism and despair. The worst thing in such cases is that suffering does not carry any meaning in itself that would soften it, making it doubly hard to bear.

Here we will endeavor to examine the question of suffering in the light of the Divine Revelation.

1. Are We Created for Sorrow or for Joy?

First of all, one thing must be clear to us: God has created us not for sorrow, but for joy. Where do we see man for the first time? In Paradise! According to the testimony of the Holy Bible, especially of the New Testament, man is intended for Paradise, not for hell. The fact that many are perishing does not yet mean that such were God's intentions for man. No! *God is Love* (I John 4:8). He does not want the death of the sinner (cf. Ezek. 33:11), but on the contrary, *will have all men to be saved and to come to the knowledge of the truth* (I Tim. 2:4). The following situation is very significant: on Judgment Day, the Saviour will say to the righteous: *Come, you blessed of My Father, inherit the kingdom prepared for you from the foundation of the world.* And He will say to the sinners: *Depart from Me, ye cursed, into everlasting fire, prepared for the devil and his angels* (Matt. 25:34, 41). From this, it is clearly seen that, according to God's plan, Paradise was prepared for men, and hell—for the demons.

2. Adam

God placed Adam in Paradise. In that wonderful place of joy the first man was unspeakably happy because he was close to God. Happiness is being with God, and away from Him there is no true or lasting joy. In the Kingdom of God where God Himself will rule, there will be no sorrow. God will wipe away every tear from the eye (cf. Rev. 7:17). Adam was happy in Paradise as long as he had an inner connection with God through grace. But where did sorrows come from?—from sin. As soon as Adam sinned he began to suffer, even though he was still in Paradise. Sin carries its own punishment in itself. The devil destroys his friends: those who obey his will. Conscience reproaches the one who goes against the divine principles and transgresses God's commandments. Even before God drove Adam out of Paradise, Adam himself had already left it inwardly by violating God's law and by losing the grace. He began to suffer from the moment he fell. It is not God, then, Who is to blame for Adam's suffering, but it is Adam himself. God had created him for joy, but he chose sorrow for himself.

3. The Christians

Some will say: "If Adam has sinned, why do we have to suffer because of him today?" We are his children and as such we must share the fate of our ancestor, but this answer treats only the objective side of the question. There is another side as well, which is subjective and explains the strength and consolation contained in our faith. We do not suffer only because of some necessity to pay for our ancestor's sin. Everyone forges his own fate, and under this circumstance we do not have to partake of all the disasters and sufferings of which Adam became a victim. If we want to, we can choose another way of life, not the way of disobedience and pride which ruined Adam, but the way of obedience and humility; and thus we can become happy even here on earth. This was somewhat possible even in Old Testament times. There have been righteous people like King David, for example, who found the lost joy of human life in their longing for God. How much more possible this is in New Testament times, after the coming of Jesus Christ Who came to earth to renew and regenerate fallen human nature, to restore to us grace and the lost paradisiacal bliss!

The Word of God testifies of the Saviour and His wondrous gifts of grace: *But as many as received Him, to them gave He the power to become the sons of God, even to them that believe on His name* (John 1:12). To become a child of God, is this not the same as returning to the lost Paradise? Is this not something even greater? This is how kind God is towards us, the children of Adam. He has given us the opportunity to avoid the disastrous fate of our ancestor if we want to. Adam was gifted by God with a free will, but he misused his freedom and transgressed God's law. That is why he began to suffer. We, too, have this great gift—freedom. If we embrace God's law, if we subject our sinful will to the holy will of God, we will not suffer like Adam but will foretaste the paradisiacal joys even in this life, and in the age to come we will also live in bliss eternally with those who have pleased God.

The saints are a proof of this. They, while still on earth, were as if in Paradise, because they were always in a mystical communion with God. They never fell away from His Law and through their humility and obedience stayed firmly in the grace which made them infinitely happy. One of the most radiant saints—St. Seraphim of Sarov—who died only about a hundred and ten years ago,[1] had achieved such a happiness on earth that it was simply overflowing the banks of his soul and attracted all who came to him in faith. For example, the Saint of Sarov greeted everyone he met with the words: "What brings you to poor Seraphim, my joy?" He was living in such a blissful and joyous state that he always felt as if it were Pascha. That is why, even during the winter, he often said to people: "Christ is risen, my joy!" St. Seraphim of Sarov also lived in a marvelous peace with all animals. An enormous bear used to come to him from the woods to eat dried bread from his hands. Does not this remind us of Adam's condition in Paradise? How much more wondrous

---

1. It has now been 161 years since St. Seraphim's death in 1833.

is this because it happens here, on earth! If things like this can happen even here, what would the condition of the righteous ones be in heaven?

4. Joy in Sorrow

Suffering in its nature is nothing else but a withdrawal from God. With God it would be well even in hell. It is known that before the death and Resurrection of Jesus Christ not one of the righteous had access to Paradise. Consequently, the righteous ones from the Old Testament who had died in faith were in hell where they awaited their salvation. Sorrow, however, did not touch them, because they were with God. In the Book of Solomon's Wisdom it is said: *But the souls of the righteous are in the hand of God, and sorrow will not touch them. They seemed dead to the eyes of the foolish ... but they abide in peace* (3:1-3). On the other hand, without God it would be terrible even in Paradise.

This is the secret of suffering—separation and withdrawal from God. If a man is with God, he is happy and he says, like the Psalmist: *For what have I in Heaven? And besides Thee, what have I desired upon earth?* (Ps. 72:23). God is the Source of joy, and the devil—the source of suffering. That is why even the sorrows which come to us according to God's will in this temporary life carry in themselves joy and lead to heavenly glory if they are endured with faith and trust in God's good providence. In contrast, the temporal sinful pleasures with which the devil tempts us carry poison in themselves, and their end is utter disappointment. Whoever follows God is happy even in suffering, as the holy Apostle Paul speaks: *sorrowful, yet always rejoicing* (II Cor. 6:10); but whoever follows the devil is unhappy even in his earthly joys. How many wicked ones there are who seem to be prospering in this world, but take a peek into their hearts. You will see such suffering, such an emptiness there!

It is true that the righteous, too, are not left without sorrows in life. The Saviour Himself has prophesied to His Apostles: *In the world ye shall have tribulation* (John 16:33). The holy Apostle Paul says directly: *All that will live godly in Christ Jesus shall suffer persecution* (II Tim 3:12). But how different those sorrows, persecutions, and sufferings for Christ and in Christ are from the sorrows of the wicked! Their sorrows lead to hopelessness and despair, and the ones in Christ—to hope and joy. The sorrows of the faithless are storms which ravage everything, but the tears of the faithful are a quiet, gracious rain which helps the beautiful flowers of virtue to grow and bloom in the soul. This is one of the extraordinary things in our precious Christian faith: **it brings joy even in suffering. It transforms the sorrows into bliss.**

When Jesus Christ was leaving this earthly life, He bequeathed to His beloved disciples sorrows and tears as if they were a most precious gift: *Verily, verily, I say unto you, that ye shall weep and lament, but the world shall rejoice* (John 16:20). He did this not to doom His beloved ones to inconsolable suffering, but to draw even more radiantly on that dark background of suffering a picture of the immeasurable bliss waiting for them. *Your sorrow shall be turned into joy* (John 16:20), He said to them, *your joy no man taketh from you* (John 16:22). Only Christ can give such an eternal happiness, a happiness which cannot be taken away. In His sermon He pronounced blessed those whom this sinful world considers to be the most wretched: blessed are the poor in spirit, blessed are the weeping, blessed are the meek, the hungry and thirsty for righteousness, the persecuted for righteousness sake, etc. To all those the Saviour said: *Rejoice, and be exceeding glad* (Matt. 5:12).

How strange! To rejoice when one is unhappy, poor, help-less, persecuted, insulted, despised, hated, slandered! Before Christ, the world did not know how to rejoice over such calamities, but now everything is reversed through the power of the God-Man. *All things work together for good to them that love God* (Rom. 8:28). For the believer, sorrow has lost its poisonous sting. Quiet hope has taken the place of the bitter despair of suffering, and suffering is not unbearably heavy any more, because it gives birth to sweet fruit. Rejoice and be glad, because sorrows are a fiery furnace in which gold is purified. Suffering is the hammer in the hand of the sculptor which makes the statue even more beautiful. Sufferings are those thorny and frightening paths which lead to sunny peaks and paradisiacal views. Rejoice and be glad! Jesus Christ Himself sanctified the road of suffering with His feet! Rejoice and be glad! *For unto you it is given in the behalf of Christ, not only to believe on him, but also to suffer for his sake* (Phil. 1:29). The Word of God calls suffering a **favor.** It is the distinction of the chosen ones of God. It is a medal of honor for the beloved of Christ.

When the holy Apostles were imprisoned for preaching the teaching of Christ, when afterwards they were judged by the Sanhedrin, beaten, and threatened so that they would stop speaking in the name of Christ, and when they were freed at last, they went out *rejoicing that they were counted worthy to suffer shame for his name* (Acts 5:41). In this way, the first Christians considered suffering for Christ to be a great honor and rejoiced in it. In the same spirit, the holy Apostles advised the faithful followers of Christ [to value suffering]. For example, the Apostle James writes: *Count it all joy when ye fall into divers temptations* (James 1:2). As St. Dimitry of Rostov teaches, the words "divers temptations" are to be understood as "all kinds of sorrows, griefs, misfortunes, persecutions, embittering diseases and adversities, impoverishment, and suffering which occur either by God's permission or by human menace, or naturally, or by chance, or by an action of the devil." In all such cases, the holy Apostles advised the Christians to rejoice and to lay their sorrow on God. What a deep and perfect understanding the first Christians had of suffering and its beneficial influence on the soul of the person who endures it patiently!

5. The Martyrs

History does not know of any more astonishing feats than those of the holy martyrs who went to die for their Redeemer with elation and with a song on their lips. Their courage and readiness to endure any kind of torture have often disarmed their tormentors, so that the latter were compelled to wonder aloud: "What is this new teaching which makes our victims joyous even amidst the deepest sorrows? What is this force which makes them love even the sufferings? What is this new and unknown God Who inspires them to such courage that they not only do not flee from death, but even desire it?!" Indeed, all this was extraordinary in the eyes of the pagans. Their braves and warriors could also be fearless in the face of death; yet, to desire death as a blessing greater than life—as a door through which one goes to God, as the holy Apostle Paul desired it (cf. Phil. 1:23)—this was terrifying and incomprehensible for the non-Christians. They could not understand the new teaching, according to which the grave is not the end of life, but a shelter from death. Just as much as this was unusual for the pagans, it was natural for the Christians whose surprising courage came from this God-revealed truth: *For whether we live, we live unto the Lord; and whether we die, we die unto the Lord: whether we live therefore, or die, we are the Lord's. For to this end Christ both*

The courageous faith of the martyrs witnessed to Christ, the Victor.
St. Lukia's martyrdom, icon from Greece.

died, and rose, and revived, that he might be Lord both of the dead and living (Rom. 14:8-9). *For He is not a God of the dead, but of the living: for all live unto Him* (Luke 20:38).

Death was filled with darkness and hopelessness for the pagans. For even though the idea of immortality had sparkled among them, too, it was not even remotely as real and joyous as the immortality which the God-Man and His Apostles reveal to us. For example, the Apostle Paul writes: *Eye hath not seen, nor ear heard, neither have entered into the heart of man, the things which God hath prepared for them that love Him* (I Cor. 2:9). Death is not frightening for the faithful and the virtuous anymore, because through it one enters into that blissful beyond where God has prepared ineffable blessings for His chosen ones. The chosen ones of God are those who have turned to God by themselves, of their own free will. These chosen ones, knowing that God has deigned to make them heirs of His Heavenly Kingdom and remembering the words of the Apostle *that the sufferings of this present time are not worthy to be compared with the glory which shall be revealed in us* (Rom 8:18), lived and died for God with joy and endured with gladness every possible kind of short-term suffering on earth for His holy Name's sake.

In the same manner, St. Seraphim of Sarov told one of the people who was spiritually close to him: "My joy! God has prepared for us such glory and bliss in heaven that if this whole room were filled with worms and they were eating our bodies and we were rotting alive, even then we should have endured all these torments with joy because of the Kingdom of Heaven!" All the saints have endured in this way with faith and hope in God's good providence. They were not scared by the temporary hardships which brought them closer to God, but were afraid only of sin which tears the soul away from grace and happiness to throw it into the abyss of eternal suffering.

6. The Faith and the Love of the Saints

Today we wonder how the saints were so consistently firm in their righteousness, how they rejoiced amid suffering, how they were determined to resist to blood (cf. Heb. 12:4) in their struggle against sin, and how they would prefer to die rather than transgress God's commandments. The courage, self-denial, and high virtues of the saints are an insoluble mystery to us, because today we do not love the Lord even remotely as ardently as they have loved Him, and because we have come to love sin in place of the Lord. If one has tasted and seen how gracious the Lord is (cf. I Pet. 2:3), he will leave everything else and constantly, with an insatiable thirst, strive towards this gracious Spring of infinite happiness.

Love towards God is a great power. If the ordinary sinful human passions are able to make a man forget all dangers and sufferings for no other reason but the satisfaction of his sinful thirst, then what heavenly strength can come over those who are burning with a seraph's love for God! For instance, the man enveloped by the passion for riches stays up whole nights thinking how to increase his riches; undertakes long and dangerous journeys across seas and mountains; suffers, frets and fumes, and endures all this heroically in the name of mammon. The man whose morbid sense of pride has been hurt wonders how to avenge himself; he is ready to demand a duel, even with the risk of dying. The man with a passion for fornication knows that he will pay with his soul for his deadly sin, but he is ready to undergo eternal torment if he could only satisfy his sinful lust. If even these earthly, sinful passions can overcome the fear of suffering, then could not love for God drive away faint-heartedness in the face of temporary sorrows?

All saints have anticipated going to the Kingdom of Heaven, have believed deeply in God, and in this faith have found the strength to rise above their human feebleness and to be empowered in the difficult exploit of the virtues. Their weaknesses and sinful inclinations were withered in the shadow of grace like grass over which a thick and mighty forest has intertwined its branches, and the comforts sent by God gave them wings to fly up closer to Him. While still in this life, they received a foretaste of the paradisiacal joys through their closeness to God. Bearing, according to the words of Christ, the Kingdom of God within themselves (cf. Luke 17:21), they considered temporary sufferings to be insignificant; they did not give in to murmuring, anger, revenge, or some other impure passion but—with the guiding help of God's grace—considered carefully in every moment how to conduct themselves so as to fulfill God's will. They preserved a marvelous peace even during the most powerful temptations, controlled their feelings, thoughts, and desires, and aimed all their spiritual powers towards virtue.

St. Seraphim of Sarov was once attacked by thieves. They had come into the woods to rob his little desert hut, thinking that they would find much money in it. After they ransacked the whole hut without finding anything, they were enraged and beat the saint so badly that he barely survived. After this beating he walked bent over for the rest of his life, but even amid this heavy suffering St. Seraphim did not stray from God's path. When the thieves were captured, he pleaded with the authorities with great persistence and tears not to punish them because of him, a sinner!

❧ Part 2 ❧

Suffering and Sin

The Expulsion of Adam and Eve from the Garden.

Suffering and Sin

7. Our Sins

IF WE COMPARE our way of responding to trials and suffering with that of the saints, we will see how far we are from their example. It was already pointed out that Adam began to suffer because he abused the free will given to him by God in subjecting it to sin. The saints did not abuse this great gift of God—their free will—but conformed their actions to God's law, and so tasted joy even in their sufferings. Today we, like Adam, constantly misuse our free will by sinning and transgressing God's commandments. This is where all our troubles come from, as well as our inability to be consoled in them.

With which of God's gifts has modern man failed to sin before God? God has given us health so that we can serve Him and our neighbors with it, but we abuse this precious gift by using it for sin and evil. God has given us riches so that we will be useful to the least of His brothers, but we misuse our riches as well. God has given us abilities in order to praise Him, yet we often bring dishonor to God's holy Name with our abilities; it is sufficient to think of those writers who use their gift to slander God and the saints. Do not the astounding contemporary achievements of technology represent the same kind of abuse of God's gifts by using them to destroy from the air entire cities and to kill peaceful citizens by the hundreds and thousands, instead of employing these achievements for increasing the well-being of mankind? We often put in service to satan all the blessings and abilities which we have received from God. Through them we seek glory and pleasures for ourselves, become proud, and harm our neighbors.

In this way we walk on the wide and deadly road which leads to hell. God, the good, loving One does not want us to perish, but to be saved and to gain a knowledge of the truth (cf. I Tim. 2:4); yet how can He save us? If His generosity towards us, His gifts, His long-suffering do not bring us to our senses and correct us, then He turns the tables. When He sees that we abuse His goodness and generosity, He begins to send us **sorrows and punishments**, so that in this way, hopefully, He would turn us to Himself.

8. God's Punishments

God is infinitely wise, good, and holy. Everything that He does is good, even the sorrows He sends for our benefit. In this life, we cannot yet fully understand that in all its depth and justice. If we could see from heaven our sinful earthly paths, if we could perceive from God's height and with His foresightedness what hellish fire we are kindling for ourselves with our evil deeds, we ourselves would agree that there are only two possibilities left for us—either to be thrown into eternal torments or to be brought to our senses, disciplined through temporary punishments and sufferings in life. Compared to the eternal torments in hell, the latter appear to be a true blessing of God, so light and easy to bear are they, so saving and necessary for our correction!

If in a school the students are extremely mischievous and do all kinds of harm, if they interfere with the education and thus are harmful both to themselves and to their classmates, would it not be injurious to the high purposes of education and for the upbringing of the children to have a teacher who faint-heartedly and good-naturedly endured all this disorder? Would it not be much better for the work if he were "worse" towards his students, i.e., if he punished the mischievous ones and thus ensured the order, good education, and discipline of the school? This whole world is an enormous school, and we are the students in it. If we are sincere, we must admit that we are very bad students—mischievous, disobedient, self-willed, and evil. When this bad behavior of ours persists, how can God teach us His holy Law if He does not send us punishments? Just as the strict teacher is good, so the punishing God is also good. When the conscientious student finishes school, he says to himself: "Thank God that our teacher was so strict and demanding. He punished us, but he taught us something." In the same way, when the believing soul comes to the end of its earthly journey, it says to the Lord with relief and gratitude: *It is good for me that Thou hast humbled me, that I might learn Thy statutes* (Ps. 118:71). Thank you, God, for punishing me and thus saving me!

Looking from on high, the sufferings which God sends to us in life are a real blessing. We are yet far from God's peaks. We are still struggling along in the lowlands of the here and now; we are still too entangled in the cares of temporary life to be able to judge accurately all the disciplinary and saving significance of suffering. Our hope is that a day will come when we will kiss the rod with which the Lord has punished us. For now though, while we are students, we still reason from this perspective and that is why our grumbling understanding of the sufferings in life is not reliable. While we are in the flesh, we value too highly our earthly benefits and interests, and we forget the soul and its eternal striving. God, Who knows that our entire earthly life will pass away like a bloom and Who teaches us that the soul—the immortal one—is the most valuable thing we have, often sends sorrows to the body in order to save the soul. In the same way, the holy Apostle Paul ordered the Corinthians to turn the man guilty of incest over to satan *for the destruction of the flesh, that the spirit may be saved in the day of the Lord Jesus* (I Cor. 5:5). If we knew how beneficial suffering is for the salvation of our souls, we ourselves would prefer it over the abundance of earthly pleasures.

Jesus Christ says: *I am the true vine, and my Father is the husbandman. Every branch in me that beareth not fruit he taketh away: and every branch that beareth fruit, he pruneth it, that it may bring forth more fruit* (John 15:1-2). **He prunes it.** What does this mean? How is the vine pruned? It is pruned by being clipped and cut. It is known that when the vine is cut, tears appear at the cuts: its branches begin to cry because they are suffering. Yet, if this vine knew that the gardener was pruning it for its own good, to protect it from barrenness, so that it would not be cut down altogether and thrown into the fire; if it could see itself in the autumn, covered with heavy, sweet grapes, it would cry out: "Blessed be the tears, blessed be the sufferings which made me so fruitful!"

9. All Grumbling is from the Devil

With such high goals God sends suffering to us, but we have a terrible enemy who seeks to turn everything good into evil: the devil. In Paradise, he lied to Adam in saying that Adam would become like God if he tasted the forbidden fruit of the tree of the knowledge of good and evil. Adam tasted it, came to know the evil, lost the good, and did not become God, but in some respects fell even lower than the animals. In this way, the devil ruined man by inspiring in him disobedience to God Who had given Adam an order not to eat from that tree. Now, when God sends to us sorrows for our good, the devil seeks to destroy that good as well, so that we will get from it not benefit but harm for our soul.

How does he work to achieve this? Sly and refined are the intrigues of the evil one. When God sends us suffering to correct us, to turn us to Himself and take us away from the evil one, the devil teaches us **to grumble** against God. Through this he keeps us under his power, even amidst the sorrows. He achieves thus a double purpose—we are suffering here because we do not have the power to eliminate our woes; and in the future, again, we will be tormented in hell because we have grumbled, and through that grumbling we have destroyed the fruits of suffering.

Grumbling is like the autumn hoarfrost which, when it falls, destroys all the labors of the gardeners. Few people realize how bad grumbling is for the soul. Almost everyone considers it to be a small sin, but even though it seems so, it has very grievous consequences. In the autumn before the hoarfrost falls, the experienced gardeners notice the signs of the coming cold weather and urge their young helpers to gather the peppers and the tomatoes. The young ones laugh: "Why should we gather them? The weather is still so nice!" Then the next morning they see that the first frost has come over the gardens. They pick up a pepper and take a bite to taste it, but it is as bitter as poison and cannot be eaten. Thus their small carelessness has destroyed all their labors. In the same way grumbling withers all the virtues of the soul and makes bitter and useless the fruits of suffering.

Often grumbling, through the devil's instigation, can grow into resentment and even blasphemy against God. Have you not seen how bedridden, suffering people who have carried their cross with great patience for a long time, suddenly, through the suggestions of the devil, begin to grumble, and to resent and even revile God? Poor people, they do not alleviate their fate. On the contrary, they aggravate it, since they will suffer both here and in the age to come because of their blasphemy against the Creator if they do not repent of this great sin. The devil has entangled them in his nets and will hold them fast until they break free from his claws by force.

10. Eulogius and the Invalid

In the wonderful book *The Lausiac History* by Bishop Palladius of Helenopol, a highly instructive story is told. A certain monk from Alexandria by the name of Eulogius was wondering which path of monastic exploit he should choose. He did not like the life in a monastery, and he could not resolve to live in seclusion. While he was thus deliberating, he saw an invalid—a man without arms and legs—lying abandoned in the market square. He only had a tongue so that he could beg from those who passed by. Eulogius stopped, observed the man for a while, and prayerfully made the following vow before God: "Lord, in Your name I will take this man with me, and I will care for him until he dies, so that I will receive salvation through him. Give me patience to serve him!" Then he approached the invalid and said: "Would you agree for me to take you with me and care for you?" The man answered: "I will come with pleasure." Eulogius put the invalid on a donkey, took him to his humble home, and bestowed good care upon him. They lived like that for fifteen years.

One day the invalid fell ill. Eulogius did everything which the sick man needed: he washed him with his own hands and gave him the appropriate good food. But after those fifteen years, some demon had come into the invalid and made him so evil that he began to curse and revile Eulogius terribly: "Go away, you wicked scoundrel! You have stolen the money of other people, and now you want to receive salvation through me. Take me back to the market square! I want to eat meat!" Eulogius gave him meat. Soon after that the invalid began to yell again: "I cannot stand this boring life any more. I want to see people. I want to be at the marketplace again. Why do you keep me here like a prisoner? Take me back to the place where you found me!" Sometimes the demon maddened him so much that he would have killed himself if he had had arms. Finally, Eulogius turned for advice to some monks and said: "What should I do? This man brings me to despair. Should I turn him out in the streets? I myself do not dare, because I made a vow before God; but he makes my whole life bitter and confuses me greatly."

They said to him: "The great one is still alive," (that is how they referred to St. Anthony the Great). "Go to him. Take a boat and the invalid with you; go to the monastery, and wait for him [St. Anthony] to come from the desert. Ask his advice and do as he says, because God speaks through him."

Eulogius did as they told him and sailed up the Nile to the monastery of St. Anthony. The latter was in the desert where he lived, but he soon came to the monastery. It was in the evening, and many people were waiting for him. The Saint came out and, even though nobody had told him the names of the visitors, called out in the darkness: "Eulogius! Eulogius! Eulogius!" However, the monk from Alexandria kept silent, because he thought that St. Anthony was calling some other Eulogius who was known to the Saint.

Anthony repeated in a louder voice: "I am speaking to you, Eulogius of Alexandria!"

Eulogius was frightened and said: "Yes, what is your wish for me?"

Anthony said: "What brings you here?"

Eulogius replied: "The One Who revealed my name to you has revealed my request to you as well."

Anthony answered: "I know why you came, but say it before all the brothers, so that they will know it, too!"

Eulogius said: "I found this invalid in the market square and made a vow before God that I would serve him in his misfortune, so that both of us would receive eternal salvation—I through him and he through me. Now, after so many years, he has begun to torment me in such an intolerable way that sometimes I think of throwing him out of my house. That is why I came to your holiness for advice on what to do."

Anthony told him sternly: "So you want to throw him out? But the One Who has created him will not throw him out! Do you really want to do that? Then God will raise another man, better than you, who will defend him." Eulogius was scared and kept quiet.

After that the Saint turned to the invalid and also rebuked him with stern words: "Wretched man, you are unfit for both the heavens and the earth! For how long will you resist God? Do you know that you are being served by Christ Himself? How do you dare to revile Christ? Did not Eulogius take on himself the obligation to serve you like a slave in the name of Jesus?"

In this way he reproved the invalid, too, and then he said to both of them: "Go in peace and do not leave each other!... God will soon take you to Himself. That is why the devil has tempted you: because you are close to the end of your lives, and you will soon receive your heavenly crowns. Do everything that you can, so that the angel of death will find you together!"

The two men went back home. Forty days later Eulogius died, and in less than three days after his death the invalid also passed away.

11. Patience and Humility

What a good moral is contained in this example! Both men were sufferers in life—the invalid suffered from an ugly deformity, and Eulogius suffered voluntarily by serving the invalid. Great reward was awaiting both of them in heaven for the patient endurance of their crosses, but the devil sought to destroy the labors of both by inciting them to grumble. That is why St. Anthony rebuked them so sternly, and then, revealing to them how close their end was, advised them to endure so that they would not lose their crowns through the devil's instigations. Indeed, with their patience they were saved.

Not grumbling, but **patience in suffering**—this is what God wants from us. *In your patience possess ye your souls* (Luke 21:19), the Saviour has instructed us, because *we must through much tribulation enter into the kingdom of God* (Acts 14:22). Into this Kingdom of God one cannot enter with pride which teaches us to grumble, but with humility which makes us patient. There are no greater teachers of patience than sorrows. This is precisely why God sends us suffering: so that we will **humble ourselves** before Him. No one has been saved by pride, because *God resisteth the proud, and giveth grace to the humble* (I Pet. 5:5). The doors of the Kingdom of Heaven are too low and narrow for the proud to enter through them; only those humbled by the sufferings of life can go through them freely.

Pride is a very loathsome sin before the Lord. The devil had not murdered or stolen, or committed adultery or some other sin of that kind. He had only become proud, and this single sin turned him from a bright angel into a dark satan. God sends us suffering to deliver us from this deadly pride. How much we should thank God for the sorrows which He sends to humble and save us! *Humble yourselves therefore under the mighty hand of God, that he may exalt you in due time* (I Pet. 5:6), says the holy Apostle Peter, and the Psalmist writes: *Blessed is the man whom thou shalt chasten, O Lord; and out of Thy law shalt Thou instruct him* (Ps. 93:12).

Through sorrows God protects us from many great troubles. Those who do not know sickness, grief, or failure become presumptuous and proud. Let us recall Napoleon Bonaparte. In the beginning of the nineteenth century he was the most famous person in the world. He conquered almost all of Europe. Nothing could stop him or impede his victorious marches; every enemy force melted before his power. Then, when he came to the walls of Moscow, blinded by his pride, he ordered that it be written on a flag: "Heaven is yours, the earth is mine!" It was from that day that Napoleon's misfortunes began. General Kutuzov defeated him before Moscow and chased the meager remnants of his armies out of Russia. Then Russian officers ordered that it be written on another flag: "The back is yours, the whip—mine!" The star of Napoleon came down from the dome of heaven, and the great conqueror finished his life in exile on the island of St. Helen. There, humbled by the hand of God, he wrote these words: "Alexander, Caesar, Carl the Great, and I founded great kingdoms; but on what did we base the creation of our genius? On power. Only Jesus based His Kingdom on love, and up to this day there are millions of people ready to die for Him."

A story is told of a very pious Russian priest who once said to one of his parishioners who was living in luxury and did not know sorrow and suffering: "God has left you, wretched man

Supplicatory prayer. Icon from the Mstislav Lectionary, Russia.

of fortune; pray to Him to send you some punishment, so that you will be delivered from your complacency and pride." Not long after that, the home of that rich man burned. He cried a lot and, pondering on the words of the good priest, accepted God's punishment with humility. That punishment was a true blessing for him, and from that day on he became a good Christian. In this way sorrow saved him. The words of Moses proved true for him: *When thou art in tribulation ... if thou turn to the Lord thy God and shalt be obedient unto his voice ... he will not forsake thee* (Deut. 4:30, 31). How much wisdom do sufferings bring in life! It is only through them that a man becomes wiser, as the Psalmist writes: *Before I was humbled, I transgressed, therefore thy saying have I kept* (Ps. 118:67).

12. Psalm 72

In the wonderful Book of Psalms, which is a tender comfort for every suffering and pious heart, there is a Psalm which works on the wounds of the soul like a balsam to numb the pain and to heal the wounds. This is Psalm Seventy-two. In it the God-inspired Psalmist gives an answer to the painful question: why do the wicked often prosper on earth and do not know sorrow, while the righteous suffer? Here are the words of the Psalmist himself:

How good is God to Israel,
To them that are upright of heart,
But as for me, my feet were all but shaken;
My steps well nigh had slipped.
For I was envious of the transgressors,
When I beheld the peace of the sinners.

For they make no sign of refusal
In the time of their death,
And they have steadfastness
In the time of their scourging.
They are not in such toils as other men,
Nor with other men shall they be scourged.
*Wherefore their **pride** hath utterly mastered them,*
They have wrapped themselves in their injustice
*   and ungodliness.*

❦ ❦ ❦

Behold, these are the sinners;
They prosper in this age and have obtained riches;
And I said: Surely in vain have I kept justice in my heart

And washed my hands among the innocent.
And I became a man scourged all the day long,
And reproof was mine in every morning.
[i.e., Was it in vain that I acted and lived piously?]

❧ ❧ ❧

And I sought to understand,
But this was too toilsome in my sight,
Until I come into the sanctuary of God
And understand their end.

This is where one can understand the secrets of life—in God's sanctuary. **The end** brings the solution of all puzzles. The wicked are spared suffering only until their deaths. It is after death that the suffering of the unrepentant sinners begins. The end determines the value of their labors! Here are some of the greatest thoughts of the inspired singer of God:

Surely, for their dealings Thou hast appointed
  evils for them;
Thou hast cast them down in their exultation.
How are they come unto desolation in a moment!
They have ceased to be;
They have perished because of their iniquity.
As a dream of one who awaketh, O Lord,
In Thy city Thou shalt bring their image to nought.

❧ ❧ ❧

For behold, they that remove themselves from Thee
  shall perish;
Thou hast destroyed all that go a-whoring from Thee.

Psalm 72:1-6, 12-14, 16-19, 25

13. The Prospering Sinners

In these God-inspired words we receive the answer to the difficult question: why do the wicked prosper? The answer is: they prosper temporarily on this earth, since they are incorrigible sinners; and the Lord has left them, because even suffering cannot set them straight. God has placed them in slippery places and takes them down into the abyss.

We know that in the wintertime children look for slippery slopes to slide down upon with their sleighs. How pleasant it is for them as they slide! They fly down like arrows, especially if there is no obstacle in their way; but how often do those who are careless fall and break heads, arms, and legs! Only then do they see how dearly this pleasure has cost them, but it is too late! It is the same way with the prosperity of the hardened and unrepentant sinners in this world. They too go down the steep path of pleasure with their sleighs of constant success, and they enjoy themselves throughout their entire life. There are no annoying obstacles for them. They fly down like arrows ... toward their peril!

If they had had branches in their way!... Surely the sticks would have annoyed and tormented them, but actually they would have been a blessing, because they would have stopped these people and protected them from going down to the bottomless pit of eternal death! If they had suffered, if their earthly existence did not consist only of songs and joys, then they might have remembered God and might have been saved. But, alas, *they make no sign of refusal in the time of their death* (Ps. 72:4). For them suffering is kept for after their death. When they die, i.e., when they wake up from their short and blissful, but false, earthly dream, they will see that all earthly goods, joys, and pleasures have disappeared like a dream. They will realize with bitterness that their bliss was illusory, but it will be too late.

❧ *Part 3* ❧

The Blessings of Suffering

If ye endure chastening, God dealeth with you as with sons....
St. Paul, by St. Andrew Rublev, 1411, Moscow.

The Blessings of Suffering

14. Suffering is a Blessing

FROM THE PREVIOUS parts of this book it is clearly seen that sufferings are a great blessing in life. Should we grumble when God sends us sorrows? We should not, rather, we should kiss the invisible Hand which punishes us. *For whom the Lord loveth, He chasteneth, and scourgeth every son whom He receiveth. If ye endure chastening,* says the holy Apostle Paul, *God dealeth with you as with sons; for what son is he whom the father chasteneth not? But if ye be without chastisement, whereof all are partakers, then are ye bastards, and not sons* (Heb. 12:6-8).

There is not one saint who has not walked the road of suffering until he was saved. St. John Chrysostom says: "Let us not consider this a sign that God has abandoned us and has despised us, when we are subjected to trials [sorrows], but let it be a sign to us that the Lord cares for us, because, by allowing the trials to come, He is cleansing our sins." God has not forgotten the man to whom He sends suffering and trials, but rather in this way He is proving His closeness to him. *The Lord is nigh unto them that are of a contrite heart, and He will save the humble of spirit. Many are the tribulations of the righteous, but the*

47

Lord shall deliver them out of them all (Ps. 34:18-19). The deeper the sorrow, the closer God is; the darker the night, the brighter the stars.

All sorrowful and humble people are God's beloved. Would God abandon them? No, He will not abandon them either in this world or in the one to come. He tenderly calls all suffering people to Himself: *Come unto Me, all ye that labor and are heavy laden, and I will give you rest* (Matt. 11:28). Even in the Old Testament He has given marvelous comfort to His beloved people: *Can a woman forget her sucking child, that she should not have compassion on the son of her womb? Yea, they may forget, yet will I not forget thee* (Is. 49:15). God speaks about every faithful son of His through the mouth of the Psalmist: *For he hath set his hope on Me and I will deliver him; I will shelter him because he hath known My name. He shall cry unto Me, and I will hearken unto him. **I will be with him in affliction, and I will rescue him** and glorify him* (Ps. 91:14-15). Is this not comforting to every suffering heart?

Christian, you who will come across these lines and will read them, be comforted in your sorrow if you are suffering! Know that God does not punish only those who have sold their souls to the devil to receive from him all earthly joys and pleasures. God does not punish only those who are not His. Like every Father, He is not concerned with the correction and upbringing of other people's children; every father punishes his own children. If God sends you trials and punishment, do not grieve inconsolably, but rejoice that you are a son of His, that He cares for your salvation! Grieve a little. This is not a sin. But grieve with faith! Shed tears, but not inconsolably! Pour out your sorrow before the Lord, but do not grumble. *Cast thy care upon the Lord, and He will nourish thee* (Ps. 54:25). *Wait on the Lord; be thou manful, and let thy heart be strengthened, and wait on the*

Lord (Ps. 26:16). Through your suffering, God is healing you and preparing you for greater future glory!

15. St. John the Merciful and the Woman

The greatest mystics of the Faith have valued suffering as a sign of the great love of God, of God's thoughtful Fatherly care which we cannot fully understand while we are in this world, but which will be seen as a blessing when viewed from the future life. Church tradition relates that St. John the Merciful, after completing a Divine Service, once noticed that a woman was crying bitterly in a corner of the church. He told his deacon: "Go and bring that woman, so that we can find out why she is so grieved: whether her husband has died, or her children are sick, or God has sent her some other misfortune."

The deacon brought the woman to the Saint. When St. John asked her why she was crying so inconsolably, she said: "How can I not cry, holy Father! Three years have passed, and no sorrow has come to us. It seems that God has forgotten us completely. There is no sickness in the home, no ox has been lost, nor has a sheep died, and my family has begun to live carelessly. I am afraid that we will perish because of our easy life, and that is why I am crying." The Bishop-Saint marvelled at that answer and praised God.

In such a way the Christians of the past have considered sufferings to be sent from God and have grieved when they did not have sorrows. If they needed trials in life so that they would not forget God and become estranged from Him, how much more necessary and saving are sufferings for us, contemporary Christians, who have sunk deeply in sins! God would not send sorrows in this life if they did not have the power to save us from eternal sorrows in hell.

16. Sufferings are a Medicine

Sufferings are bitter medicines with blessed effects. They cure our various sins, especially pride, and humble us. When the doctor treats a sick man, he does not give him sweet dainties, but medicines which are usually bitter. If the sick man is wise, he accepts these bitter drugs with gratitude and without grumbling, knowing that they will cure him. Only foolish children make faces and do not want to drink the saving medicines because they are bitter to the tongue! How much we resemble foolish children when we grumble against the sufferings and sorrows in life which God sends to us! In our times of deepest grief, we must remember righteous Job who suffered without guilt and, despite that, accepted all misfortunes which piled upon him without grumbling and blaspheming. He lost his property, his herds, his servants, and even his children. One after the other came the messages which informed him of the woes which had come upon him. At receiving every tragic piece of news, he only repeated the wonderful words: *The Lord gave, and the Lord hath taken away; blessed be the name of the Lord. In all this, Job sinned not, nor charged God foolishly* (Job 1:21-22).

17. Patience to the End

Through his sufferings, Job received salvation. However, not all suffering is beneficial to the soul and elevates it, taking it into the Heavenly Kingdom. It is only that suffering which is endured patiently, with gratitude and trust in God, and without grumbling. Those who suffer must have great patience, so that they will be able to see how the bitter green buds on the branches of the virtuous life slowly and gradually, under the care of the warm Sun of righteousness, ripen and turn into sweet fruits of perfection and salvation. Those who suffer must have great patience lest they despair and, because of their impatience, the fruits fall before their due time—sour, bitter, and green. In such a case their suffering is in vain. Only *he that shall endure unto the end shall be saved* (Matt. 24:13). According to the teaching of St. Ephraim the Syrian, "The Christian must stand among the various sorrows and temptations like an anvil which, even though it is constantly hammered upon, does not move from its place, nor does it get ruined, but stays the same [as firm as it was in the beginning]."

We cannot be saved without suffering; how else could we be tested by God for being firm and unwavering in virtue? God arranges many things in life in such a way that man is tempted, so that his free will can be manifested, and he, through the enduring of all trials, can receive salvation. "Because those," according to the words of St. Macarius the Great, "who live in suffering and temptations and endure to the end will not lose the Kingdom of Heaven."

It is told about a saint that he, like the holy Apostle Paul, was seized and taken to heaven where he saw the bright homes of the righteous. He stopped in front of a wondrous palace in which a righteous and blissful soul was shining, and he asked: "What were you on earth?" It answered: "I was a leper, and I constantly thanked God for that mercy." Such are the fruits of sufferings which are borne with gratitude and without grumbling.

Some are bothered by the thought that their suffering may be pointless and fruitless for the salvation of their souls. They tell themselves: the saints endured for Christ's sake, and that is why they were certain that through the enduring of suffering they would save their souls. But we, unlike the saints, suffer either for our sins, or because of the envy of evil people, or by some chance; and because we do not suffer for Christ's sake, our sufferings weigh us down with their aimlessness and torment us doubly because of their uselessness. To this we should answer that nothing in this world happens by chance—without God's will or God's permission. Even a single hair does not fall from our heads without God's knowledge (cf. Luke 21:18). If we are suffering because of our own sins but we endure and repent before God, these sufferings free us from future punishment in the life beyond the grave and save us. The thief who was saved was crucified for his sins on a cross on the right side of Christ; but through his endurance and repentance, he entered Paradise.

Suffering is to the soul what fire is to ore. Ore, mixed with dirt, gravel, and other things, is purified when it passes through fire. The soul, muddied by sins, clears up when it passes patiently through sufferings. Even though the sinner does not suffer like the martyrs for Christ's sake, these woes of his are counted as sufferings for God's sake and are beneficial to him when he is consumed with a yearning to be saved, humbles himself in his sorrows, repents of his sins, and says: "For my lawlessness, I deserve much greater sufferings than the merciful God has sent me." St. John Chrysostom says that "the soul is cleansed when it suffers sorrows for God's sake." Muddy water cannot be made clear unless it passes through the filter of sand. In the same way, the soul cannot be cleansed unless it goes through sufferings.

If we undergo troubles without guilt, from the malice of evil people, then, according to the words of St. Dimitry of Rostov, even though we are not enduring persecution because of Christ, our sorrows will be counted as suffering for Christ's sake and will bring us martyrs' crowns if we give thanks to God and do not grumble. Thus every suffering can become suffering for God's sake.

18. St. Ephraim the Syrian

But who among us today can boast that he is suffering without guilt? Is not every one of our misfortunes a just punishment for our open or hidden lawlessness, our conscious or involuntary sins, for our sins are so many! If God does not punish us right away, it is because He is waiting for us to repent. It is when He sees that we do not intend to repent that He sends us punishments. We often think that we are suffering unjustly, but if we examine the matter more closely, we will find our guilt.

Once St. Ephraim the Syrian was travelling to a city. On the way, he stopped in a village and dropped in to spend the night in the house of an old woman, a widow, who was a very good Christian and whom he had known from before. The widow welcomed him very well, treated him to the milk of the only cow she had, and saw him off in the morning. In the city, St. Ephraim found a great bustle: it was a market day. He mingled with the crowd to see what was being sold. Here one man was praising his goods, there another was yelling, and farther on, a third one was bargaining noisily with his customers.... Suddenly a line of guards surrounded a group of people, and St. Ephraim happened to be one of them. They were all taken to the jail. It turned out that these were thieves who had come down from the mountains, mixed with the people, and were planning to carry out some robberies among the noise and havoc of the marketplace; but the guards found out about it and stopped them in time.

In the dark and humid room of the jail the thieves yelled, cursed, and nervously moved to and fro. St. Ephraim stood quietly in a corner, away from them, and humbly prayed to God, wondering why this misfortune had befallen him. Without anyone noticing him, he spoke with God prayerfully and, with pain in his soul, asked him: "Lord, why did You bring me into this dungeon? These people had it coming; it is because of their deeds that they were caught and imprisoned, but I ... why?" St. Ephraim prayed and cried like this for a long time. At last he fell asleep. In that sleep he heard a voice: "Do you remember that when you were in the home of the poor widow and you were going out, you forgot to close the gate? The widow's cow was in the yard. It went out through the gate and got lost. The poor woman was supporting herself with this cow. That is why God allowed you to be caught, too!" St. Ephraim was startled and woke up. He remembered that all had happened the way it was described in the dream. Then he lifted his hands towards heaven, praised God, and thanked Him for being punished justly for an unintentional and unnoticed sin....

How numerous are our unintentional sins! And how many are the voluntary ones! If one unintentional sin of St. Ephraim was not left unpunished, will God spare us with all of our willful transgressions? Our sins are so many that we deserve to be eternally tormented in hell for them, but the kind-hearted God has thought of a way to make us fit for Paradise. He sends us sufferings, the short-lived sorrows in our temporary life, and He wants us to endure them repentantly and without grumbling. God even mixes joys with the troubles and eliminates the bitterness of the sorrows with the sweetness of heavenly comforts, but we complain even then! If we could see the whole horror of our sins, we would tremble and thank God for His lenience, having realized that *not according to our iniquities hath He dealt with us, neither according to our sins hath He rewarded us* (Ps. 102:9).

Elder Ambrose of Optina.

19. The Right and Left Sides

To those who despite all this are still bothered by the thought that they are suffering without guilt, the great Elder of Optina, Fr. Ambrose, gave a wonderful instruction. Interpreting the words of the Saviour: *But whosoever shall smite thee on thy right cheek, turn to him the other also* (Matt. 5:39), he reasons: usually a man strikes with his right hand, so that the strike falls on the left cheek of the man. But Christ says: *But whosoever smites thee on thy right cheek....* Could He, the Omniscient, have not realized this common detail? Of course not! Yet if He has said: *But whosoever smites thee on thy right cheek,* then undoubtedly He had in mind to reveal to us a great divine wisdom. The right-hand side is always a symbol of good, of the right thing, and the left-hand—of evil, of the wrong thing. *But whosoever smites thee on thy right cheek* means: if someone is hurting you when you are in the right, when you are innocent, *turn the other to him also; i.e., turn your left cheek, remember your wrongdoings and sins, and your indignation at having to suffer unjustly will subside.*

20. St. Macarius the Egyptian

According to the teachings of the Word of God and the Holy Fathers, even if it happens that we suffer entirely without guilt, we should not give in to despondency, but on the contrary—we should rejoice. *For this is thankworthy, if a man for conscience toward God endure grief, suffering wrongfully. For what glory is it if, when you are buffeted for your faults, ye shall take it patiently? But if when ye do well and suffer for it, ye take it patiently, this is acceptable with God* (I Pet. 2:19-20). The greatest example of unjust suffering is Jesus Christ Himself, Who *[left] us an example, that ye should follow His steps* (I Pet. 2:21). In the lives of the saints there also are many moving descriptions of innocent sufferings which were endured with unparalleled patience in Christ's name. If someone wants to comfort his heart with such examples, he should read about the lives of St. Poemen the Long-suffering—a saint of the Kiev Caves (commemorated August 7th)—and of the holy St. Dulas (commemorated June 15th). Here we are going to mention only one example from the life of the great man of God, St. Macarius.

St. Macarius lived as a monk in a cave near the city of Alexandria, and there he wove baskets and prayed to God all day long. A pious Christian used to come to him—he was his only connection with the city. He took the products of St. Macarius' hands to Alexandria, sold them there, and with the money he bought dried bread and other supplies for the saint. In this way, St. Macarius lived quietly and unobtrusively. However, the man who supplied him with food was constantly boasting among his acquaintances in the city: "Ah, what a man I know—a true angel in the flesh! How holy he lives! And how he works!..."

A great storm soon thundered over the quiet cave of St. Macarius. A certain young woman in the city was found with child. When her parents noticed this after some time, they were worried greatly and asked her: "Why did you bring such shame to our home? With whom did you sin?" The girl was ashamed and did not want to expose the man who was to blame, and, in order to shield him, she said: "The hermit over there, Macarius, he did this to me." The parents were appalled and shocked to the bottom of their souls. Soon the whole city heard of what Macarius was said to have done. The people surrounded his helper and began to reproach him: "You were boasting that Macarius was a saint, but see what he has done. He dishonored a maiden. He is not a saint, but a liar and a hypocrite!" The helper lowered his head and did not know what to say, but he could not believe that the meek and God-fearing monk Macarius could have committed such a grave sin.

The indignant relatives of the young woman went to Macarius, dragged him out of his cave by force, brought him to the city, and led him through the busiest streets to revile and expose him before all. The poor Macarius, disturbed by this trial which had come to him so suddenly, surrendered himself to God's will and decided not to defend himself, but to endure everything for the Lord's sake. The city became very lively. As St. Macarius was led through the most crowded streets, there were whispers and mockery at the expense of the defenseless monk. The people winked at each other and laughed. Some threw stones at him, and others came near and spat in his face. Thus St. Macarius, with a lowered head, walked dishonored and reviled by all, praying secretly to God.

In the evening, the city court decided: Macarius would support both the girl and the child when it was born. The Saint went back to his cave, and, when he was left alone, he began to weave baskets again. He wove and prayed to God for a long time. At last, the time for sleep came, and St. Macarius began to cry and to talk to himself: "Macarius, Macarius, now you cannot sleep as much as you used to before. From now on you will have to work twice as much because you have to support a woman, and a child is coming, too." He never protested and patiently carried the heavy and shameful cross allotted to him by God, paying the support of the woman regularly every week, because such was the order of the city court, but the court of God did not decide so. The Lord soon showed the innocence of His servant.

When the time came for the young woman to give birth, she had pain and the hours were passing, but she could not deliver the child. Several days passed in great anguish, and she was facing certain death. Then the girl realized that she was suffering because she had slandered an innocent man, and she repented before God, confessed everything, and announced who was truly to blame. Immediately, she was delivered, but her parents and relatives who were around her were greatly disturbed and frightened. They all began to regret that they had dishonored an innocent man so cruelly. Everyone wondered at his patience. His feat suddenly grew to enormous proportions in their eyes as they remembered how he bore his shame without protest, how he allowed himself to be mocked and slandered, and how he did not defend himself. They then decided to go to him to ask for forgiveness.

When St. Macarius' helper heard of this, he was greatly cheered and ran before everyone else to the Saint's cave where he found the monk quietly weaving baskets and praying. He called: "Rejoice, Father Macarius! Your innocence was revealed!" He explained everything then, telling the Saint that people were coming from the city to apologize to him. St. Macarius, instead of rejoicing, cried: "Woe is me, for I have lost my heavenly reward!" He ran away and hid in another place, so that he would not be praised by the people.

This is how wonderful the exploits of the saints were in suffering! Among sorrows their heavenly crowns shone even more brightly. They became holier as they were bathed with their own tears. If they endured so courageously even the hardships to which they were subjected without guilt, what can we now say about ourselves when we suffer for our numerous sins and grumble despite that? We must not complain, but marvel at God's mercy which seeks to make us fit for Paradise through temporal sufferings. *For whom the Lord loveth He chasteneth, and scourgeth every son whom He receiveth* (Heb. 12:6). God tests us and punishes us here a little, so that He can accept us in His Heavenly Kingdom. Temporal sufferings deliver us from eternal ones, even though the first are incomparably smaller than the second; but in this God's wisdom and kindness are expressly shown. Knowing this, many saints have prayed to God to punish them here, in this short life, so that He would pardon them in the eternal one. St. Ephraim the Syrian has spoken: "Punish me here, my Saviour, and pardon me there!" But we want to live in joy and pleasure only, both here and in the life to come, and that is impossible.

Let us imagine that God tells us to choose one of the two: either to suffer for one day so that we will be healthy and happy for the rest of our lives, or to rejoice and feast for only one day and be unhappy and sick from then on. What would we choose? The first offer, undoubtedly—to be in suffering only one day and live with joy for the rest of our life. Is it not the same way with our life now? Our earthly existence is like a day in comparison to eternity. How much better it is to suffer here a little and to endure our sorrows without grumbling, so that we will be in the place of joy in the world beyond! St. John Chrysostom, amazed at the mercifulness of God's will for us, says: "He has determined toils for here where life is short, and He has kept the crowns for the future where life is eternally young and unending!"

21. One Hour in Hell

Bishop Theophan the Recluse gives a very instructive example which vividly illustrates the truth that the sufferings which are endured without grumbling on earth free the sinful soul from the eternal torments in the world to come. A certain man was seriously ill for years and endured everything courageously; but when his body began to rot, he could not stand the great pain and the terrible stench and cried: "Lord! I cannot endure any more! Take my soul!" An Angel of the Lord appeared to him immediately and said: "God has heard your prayer. But since, according to His just judgment, you have one year left to suffer on earth in order to be completely cleansed from your sins, He will let you choose to either suffer in sickness for one more year on earth, or for your soul to be taken to hell for three hours only." The sick man thought: "A whole year of suffering on this bed! This is unbearable! No, it is better to be in hell for three hours." So the Angel took his soul, locked it in hell, and left it alone (there).

With the departure of the Angel, the last light disappeared from that terrible place of anguish. The ill man heard only the hopeless wailing of the sinners being tormented in the eternal fire, saw the mean faces of the demons flashing before him, and, as he felt lonely and abandoned by all, began to call desperately, but only the deaf echo of the hellish abyss answered his cries. No one came to help him, because there all sinners are preoccupied with their own sorrows. Thus this poor man began to suffer intolerably himself. The minutes passed like hours, the hours like days, and the days like years. It seemed to him that he had been suffering for ages in the dungeon of hell, and he despaired that he would ever be rescued from that place of torment. Finally, he began to groan and cry with all his strength.

At last a quiet light appeared above him, and the Angel appeared. "How do you feel here, brother?" he asked.

The man could barely answer through his agony: "I did not think that an Angel would lie to me."

"How is that?" asked the Angel.

The man continued, "You promised me that you would take me away from here after only three hours, and whole ages have passed in these torments!"

"Ages?" answered the Angel with a quiet smile. "Only one hour has passed, and you have to stay here for two more."

"Two more hours?" cried the man fearfully. "Only one hour has passed? Oh, I cannot endure this any longer! I have no strength left! If there is God's mercy for me, please take me away from here! It is better for me to suffer for years and centuries on earth. I am even ready to suffer there until the Second Coming, just take me out of here!"

The Angel then said: "It is good that God let you suffer in hell, so that you could see from what sufferings He, in His love, seeks to save you with your temporal pains, so that, as you come to know this, you will not grumble in your suffering." At these words the man opened his eyes, having awoken in his body after an hour of unconsciousness; and from that day on, he began to endure with **pleasure** his grave illness, which now seemed to him insignificant and light in comparison to the torments in hell.

❧ Conclusion ❧

SUFFERING READERS! You who read these lines, learn from the words of God quoted here and from the wondrous examples of the holy righteous ones of God. You are not alone in your suffering. Hear the promise of the Lord: *I am with him in affliction* (Ps. 91:15). *The Lord is nigh unto them that are of a contrite heart, and He will save the humble of spirit* (Ps. 34:18). *Wherein ye greatly rejoice, though now for a season, if need be, ye are in heaviness though manifold temptations* (I Pet. 1:6). Do your best not to grumble! Remember the patience of Job and David's humility! It is not without reason that sorrows are being sent to us on earth. Suffering *yieldeth the peaceable fruit of righteousness unto them which have been exercised thereby* (Heb. 12:11). The word of God testifies: *For our light affliction, which is but for a moment, worketh for us a far more exceeding and eternal weight of glory* (II Cor. 4:17). Remember that God is Love and that He loves you most when He punishes you, because through punishments He shows His concern for you and seeks to save you. That is why He also *will not suffer you to be tempted above that ye are able, but will with the temptation also make a way to escape, that ye may be able to bear it* (I Cor. 10:13). Glory be to Him, the God Who is loving to us even through punishment, glory to Him through the ages! Amen.

VOLUME III

Strife & Reconciliation

BY ARCHIMANDRITE SERAPHIM ALEKSIEV

Translated by Ralitsa Doynova

Cain and Abel, from the original Bulgarian text of
Strife & Reconciliation.

I

Strife

For if ye forgive men their trespasses, your heavenly Father
will also forgive you: but if ye forgive not men their trespasses,
neither will your Father forgive your trespasses.

Matthew 6:14-15

STRIFE among people is one of the great evils of this life. It ruins brotherly relations among men and makes enemies out of friends. If you ask: "Why do these neighbors not speak to each other?" you usually hear, "They quarreled!" If you ask: "Why do these friends not greet each other?" you are answered, "They quarreled!" If you ask, "Why do these relatives not visit one another?" the same answer follows, "They quarreled!" You probably have known or know two nice families, both of which are composed of very kind people of themselves, but they cannot stand each other. The demon of strife has come between them and does not let them be reconciled and live in peace. Satan's instigation is the original cause of all dissension and discord. How many people today take each other to court and waste time and money, and lose their peace because of revenge. Again, if you ask, "Why are they suing each other?" you will hear, "They have quarreled, exchanged hurtful words, and do not want to forgive...."

This is happening also among Orthodox Christians, among brothers in the Faith whom Jesus Christ Himself united through His divine teaching, and for whom He hung on the cross to redeem and save! This is happening among followers of Christ who have received from their Heavenly Teacher the legacy: *A new commandment I give unto you, that ye love one another; as I have loved you, that ye also love one another. By this shall all men know that ye are my disciples, if ye have love one to another* (John 13:34-35). Today, where is this love which should be among us?

We have one dedicated enemy—the devil. Is he not enough (for us), but we make enemies out of our brothers in the faith, too? When the devil seduces us to be hostile, he makes us even worse than himself, because a demon never opposes another demon. Yet under the pressure of satan's malice, human turns against human, Christian against Christian, and brother against brother.

Bandits when they unite become friends. Their common goals and interests bring them closer. They break bread together at meals and respect each other as brothers, but we Christians, supposedly pursuing the highest common goal—the salvation of our souls—and lining up at the same spiritual Meal to partake from the same cup of the Body and Blood of God, in reality fight among ourselves like ferocious beasts and are far worse than bandits. It is so because we have allied ourselves with the devil. When the devil becomes our friend, we begin to quarrel with people. Therefore, if we want to be reconciled with our human enemies again, we must quarrel with the devil.

Of course, in life as it is now, it is impossible to have perfect and lasting peace. It is natural, considering our sinfulness, that discord and quarrels appear among people; but that does not mean that once having quarreled we should remain in perpetual strife. We have sinned! We have quarreled! Now, let us be reconciled!... Unfortunately, few are those who make peace after a fight and return to living like brothers. Even fewer are those who forgive their irreconcilable enemies from the heart and put up with them. Too often strife remains among people to grow and gain strength until it brings them a harvest of eternal death. There are then three kinds of relations possible between those who have quarreled: 1) strife, 2) mutual reconciliation, and 3) long-suffering and forgiveness for the enemy who may be irreconcilable.

Let us first look at the case of mutual animosity.

Why do people usually quarrel?—for being insulted by hurtful words, because of rumors and slander, for posts and jobs, for money and property, pre-eminence and honors. Whatever the reasons for the quarrel may be, the animosity created by it begins to poison the soul unrelentingly. The poor man once having surrendered to strife loses sweet spiritual peace and is tormented by malice and helpless anger. He becomes restless and nervous, and burns with a satanic hatred; happiness leaves his heart. He seeks a way to get revenge and thinks that he will regain peace only after destroying his enemy. This, however, is only one of the devil's lies: the evil one is inducing him to commit more and more crimes which fail to give him peace and make him even more miserable. When looked at from the outside, the cup of anger seems full with a drink promising satisfaction; but when we drink it, the intoxicating liquid only stuns us for a moment until we carry out the revenge, and afterwards it may lead us to despair and moral exhaustion.

Thus, once deceived by the devil, one seems powerless to overcome his anger and again seeks to be drunk with its giddiness, finding some perverted pleasure in the deep sorrow which anger brings. If anger is not uprooted in time—while it is still a small sapling with weak fibers in the earth—it is not easy to be defeated later, when it becomes a large tree with strong roots; then it turns into incurable satanic venom. This is why the Word of God advises: *Let not the sun go down upon your wrath: neither give place to the devil,* (Eph. 4:26-27); otherwise, if you once lose control of the fire, you will never be able to put it out. St. Tikhon of Zadonsk says, "Just as fire if it is not extinguished quickly will swallow many houses, so anger if it is not stopped right away, will do great harm and will cause many troubles."[1]

If the quarreling man does not turn away from that deadly road in time, he, under the pressure of his anger, can kill or cripple his enemy, take away or harm his property or his health, hurt his children and relatives, slander and dishonor him, etc., etc. It is peace for himself which the man is seeking in all of these evil deeds, but he only finds new sorrows and worries. Where there is malice there is no peace. How many neighbors begin their quarrels over very insignificant things and then, once incited by the devil to hate, cannot forgive one another? Thus quarrels poison their whole lives. As a spark can set entire forests on fire, so even the smallest quarrel can cause irremediable calamities. The cases are not rare when two neighboring families begin a fight over a hand's breadth of land from their fields or an egg laid by one family's hen in the other's yard. They continue the disagreements by adding to the initial reasons other, greater ones, pouring oil on the fire, and, instead of putting it out while it is still small, they kindle it more and more. Insulting each other in bitter rows, they come to hate one another with a devilish hatred and begin to harm each other in whatever way they can—either by damaging the other's prop-

---

1. *Works,* p. 205.

erty or by suing each other. Often, such people end in bank-ruptcy, but the worst thing is the moral harm which they do to their own souls. If they go that far, reconciliation between them becomes almost unthinkable [to them].

How wonderful it would be to stop the quarrel in time! How many sins would be prevented! How much tension would be avoided! I know, dear readers, how once a terrible fight would have occurred between two neighbors if wisdom had not pre-vailed in one of them. The occasion for the quarrel was again a petty one. One of the women had a hen with ten little yellow chicks, and the other one had a flower garden on which she doted. Once the hen with her chicks had come into the flower garden and had begun to peck between the plants. When the mistress of the garden saw that she flew into a rage, came out of her house, and started throwing rocks at the birds, who took to flight. The chicks were small and passed easily through the fence, but the hen could not find a place to escape, and so she fluttered about seeking her scattered children. This went on for quite a while. In the end, the exhausted hen almost fell to the ground with fatigue. Meanwhile, the owner of the chickens came out of her house, found out what was happening, and in her turn was enraged. She was ready to quarrel with the cruel tormentor of the chicks, but others held her back. Finally, the hen came home, and the chicks gathered around her; all ended well. Many years have passed since then; the chicks and the hen have filled their masters' pots. The woman with the garden has passed away. Now I hear the owner of the hen only say as she recalls that incident: "Thank God that people stopped me from fighting! Otherwise, the quarrel with my reposed neighbor would still be weighing upon me. Now everything is forgotten; everything has disappeared, but the sin would have remained. Thank God, thank God that we did not fight!"

Dear readers, are not all of our fights based on events similar to the petty and silly incident just described? How many people who have lived before us on this earth have quarreled over earthly and transient things: houses and lands, money and honors, insults and slanders. Why did all of this happen? What is the use of their having shown obstinacy and even a kind of heroism in their fights? These people have long since died, and their feuds are forgotten by the generations that followed. Only the sin remains to accuse at the Last Judgment the deceased who have died unrepentant of their animosity and to deprive them of the eternal joys of Paradise which are promised to the merciful, the meek, the peacemakers, and the righteous.

The sin of strife ruins both this life and the life beyond. It is an enemy to both our body and our soul. How is it, then, that some people seek comfort in quarrels and revenge? Why do they say, "I will not *rest* until I am avenged?"

Is it possible, man, for your conscience to be pacified and to bring you spiritual peace while you are burdening it with new and grave sins? Is it possible for a boat to lighten when you are loading it with more weight? You are looking for repose and peace? You will find them not in revenge, but in putting an end to strife. You are looking for coolness amid the swelter of your passions? Why then do you feed the fire of hatred and add new wood to it? You are seeking to satisfy your heart in its thirst for peace? Why then do you poison it with the bitter water of lawlessness? If you forgive your neighbor, the fire of hatred will die out in your soul, and the blessed breeze of peace will cool and refresh you. If you forget the sins of your neighbor, God will forget your sins also by erasing them from your conscience. Forgive, and you will be forgiven!

Put an end to your strife, and the sun of joy will rise in your heart! You will not find the desired peace and satisfaction in quarrels and revenge, just as a thirsty man cannot quench his thirst with salty sea water. The more you fight and become embittered, the deeper you descend into hell. And what happiness can you find in hell?! Wretched captive of strife, beware whom you are serving with your quarrels! The devil is deceiving you in order to cast you into the abyss. God will condemn to eternal torment those who, like you, are stubbornly fighting with their neighbors. This is why the Savior is advising you: *Agree with thine adversary quickly, whiles thou art in the way with him; lest at any time the adversary deliver thee to the judge and the judge deliver thee to the officer, and thou be cast into prison* (Matt. 5:25).

Fatal is the spiritual condition of the man who ages with malice and strife. He reaches an extent of bitterness which equals spiritual death. Such a man is implacable and incorrigible. The wildest and most ferocious beasts submit more easily to taming than he. If this man persists in his bitterness to the end, God will take His grace away from him and, since he cannot be corrected, He will send him to the hell which the man himself has chosen. He has been merciless towards others and thus has become unworthy of God's mercy. He has not forgiven, and that is why he cannot be forgiven. The holy Apostle James writes: *For he shall have judgment without mercy, that hath shown no mercy....* (Jam. 2:13).

War. From Novgorod Archives, Russia, 15th century.

II

Punished Stubbornness

THE FOLLOWING EXAMPLE shows how God punishes obstinate bitterness. In the monastery of Kiev Caves there lived a hieromonk by the name of Titus. He and the deacon Evagrius loved each other very much and got along very well. Everyone marveled at their sincere friendship, but the devil then embroiled them so badly that they could not stand each other. When one of them was incensing in church, the other one ran away from the incense; and even if he could not escape in time, the first one did not cense him. A long time passed and they lived constantly in this sinful darkness, and thus irreconciled dared to take Communion. The brothers pleaded with them to make peace, but they would not hear of it.

It was God's providence that the presbyter Titus should fall fatally ill. He then began to cry bitterly for his sin and sent people to ask the deacon Evagrius for forgiveness on his behalf. The deacon not only did not forgive him, but he cursed him with bitter words. The brothers, when they saw that Titus was already in agony, brought Evagrius by force to reconcile them. The sick man stood up with great difficulty, fell at the feet of the deacon, and begged him with tears in his eyes: "Forgive me, Father!" But Evagrius callously turned his face away from him and said: "I do not want to forgive him either here or in the life to come!"

As he said these words, he tore himself from the hands of the brothers and fell to the ground. They wanted to lift him up, but they found him dead. At the same time, the blessed Titus was immediately healed. Everyone was terrified by the occurrence and began asking Titus what it meant. Then he told them what he had seen with his spiritual eyes: "When I was ill and I did not give up my anger towards my brother, I saw that the angels were withdrawing from me and were crying over the death of my soul and that the demons were rejoicing at my anger. That is why I asked you to go to the brother and implore him for his forgiveness for me. When you brought him to me, and I bowed before him and he turned away from me, I saw an angel who was holding a fiery spear and who struck the unforgiving one with it. Immediately, he fell dead. But to me the same angel gave his hand and helped me up, and here I am healthy again." [1]

How often in life it happens that embittered and ir-reconciled Christians suddenly leave this world and set out for the kingdom of eternity with anger in their souls! What pardon can they expect from God if they themselves have not forgiven those who have sinned against them?! It is terrible to live irreconciled, but it is even worse to die irreconciled! Bitterness and strife make the soul unfit to bear divine grace, and thus they destroy it.

Here is one more example from the Lives of the Saints. In the first centuries of Christianity when the followers of Christ were cruelly persecuted by the authorities, a priest by the name of Sapricius and a layman by the name of Nicephorus lived in the city of Antioch. The other people considered them to be natural brothers because they loved each other so much. They lived with sincere love for a long time until the devil, being very

---

1. *Lives of Saints,* February 27.

jealous of their harmonious life, succeeded in planting the seed of strife between them. Under his influence they quarreled, were separated, and came to hate each other so much that they did not even want to meet each other on the road. After living like this for quite a while, Nicephorus came to his senses and, when he realized that their mutual hatred came from the devil, asked some of his friends and neighbors to go to the priest Sapricius and to ask him for forgiveness. Sapricius, however, did not forgive him, and Nicephorus repeated his attempt for reconciliation. He then sent people for the third time, but it was all in vain—Sapricius hardened his heart and remained implacable. At last Nicephorus himself went to Sapricius, fell at his feet, and humbly began to beg: "Forgive me, Father, for God's sake, forgive me!" Sapricius did not even look at him, and Nicephorus went away from him disgraced and rejected.

At this time, an unexpected persecution against the Christians broke out in Antioch. The more distinguished Christians were arrested first, and Sapricius, being a priest, was among them. When they brought him before the governor for questioning and asked him what his name was, he said: "Sapricius."

"And from what family are you?" the governor asked him.

"I am a Christian," was the firm reply.

"Are you a clergyman?" asked the governor again.

"I am a priest," said Sapricius.

Then the governor said: "Our king, the ruler of this land, ordered all Christians to sacrifice to the gods. And whoever does not obey the king's order must know that he will be sentenced to death after various tortures."

Sapricius stood before the ruler and without flinching answered:

"We Christians, O governor, have Christ as King, because He alone is a true God and Creator of the heavens, the earth, the sea, and everything that is in them. And all the gods of the pagans are demons."

At these words the governor was enraged and ordered that Sapricius be tortured very cruelly. The sufferer endured all tortures bravely and said to the governor: "You have power over my body but not my soul. Only my God, Jesus Christ Who has created it, has power over it."

The judge, when he saw Sapricius' firmness, sentenced him to death by beheading, and the martyr was led to the place of his execution.

In the meantime, Nicephorus heard about all of this, ran out of his home, intercepted Sapricius on the road, fell at his feet, and began to implore him:

"Martyr of Christ, forgive me! I have sinned against you."

Sapricius did not answer. His heart was still filled with demonic spite. The humble Nicephorus hurried along another street, again intercepted Sapricius, and implored him:

"Martyr of Christ, forgive me! As a human I sinned against you. Now you are being given a heavenly crown by Christ, because you confessed His Holy name before many witnesses."

Sapricius, blinded by hatred, remained implacable. Even his tormentors wondered at his obstinacy and bitterness and spoke to Nicephorus:

"We have never seen such a crazy man as you. This one is going to his death, but you are asking him so persistently for forgiveness! Can he harm you even after his death? Why do you need to make peace with him?"

Nicephorus replied: "You do not know what I am asking of the confessor of Christ, but God knows."

When they came to the place where Sapricius was to be beheaded, Nicephorus again said to him: "I beg you, martyr of Christ, forgive me!"

Nicephorus begged for a long time, but Sapricius did not have pity on him. God then took away His grace from Sapricius, and he immediately fell away from Christ. When his tormentors told him to bow down so that they could cut off his head, he suddenly became afraid and cried: "Do not kill me! I will do everything that the king orders. I will bow to the gods, and I will sacrifice to them." Thus Sapricius lost God's grace, and his salvation with it, because of his spite. Neither the endured tortures nor the admonitions of the good Nicephorus not to deny Christ at the end of his feat helped. Then the Blessed Nicephorus confessed before the executioners that he was a Christian and that he, like the rest of those who believed in Christ, did not and would not sacrifice to the gods; and he asked that he be killed in the place of Sapricius. After consulting the governor, the tormentors let Sapricius go free and killed the Blessed Nicephorus.

Thus Sapricius fell away from Christ and passed away in his malice. Nicephorus was honored with martyrdom and was saved.[2]

When we hear of the behavior of the inexorable Sapricius, we unwittingly remember the wondrous words of the holy Apostle Paul: *And though I bestow all my goods to feed the poor, and though I give my body to be burned, and have not charity, it profiteth me nothing* (I Cor. 13:3). Even martyrdom without love does not save. Even though you may have carried out the greatest of feats, if you are irreconcilable to your personal enemies, you are destroying all your good deeds and dooming yourself to death.

---

2. *Lives of Saints,* February 9.

St. Tikhon visiting prisoners.
Illustration from *Russky Palomnik*, 1903.

III

Boastful Malice

How can this strange phenomenon be explained: many people, bitter against their neighbors and seeking revenge, not only are not ashamed of their slavery to the devil but even boast of it? This can be explained in only one way—as the hopeless moral blindness of the embittered.

"It is a great folly," says St. Tikhon of Zadonsk, "for a man to boast of that for which he should mourn!" This shows how gravely the divine principles are perverted in the conscience of those who are quarreling. To rejoice over that for which only the demons are glad, to boast of that for which the angels are crying, to cheer for having buried brotherly love, to be comforted by having fulfilled the devil's desire—does not all of this show a demonic state of soul? Those who have slipped into the ditch of quarrels and rows should repent deeply, not boast of it! Speaking of the spiritual perversion of the quarreling, St. Tikhon sadly says:

> They have harmed their neighbor and trampled on the holy and divine law; they have angered God, the great and awesome Creator, written their names on the list of satan, and have destined themselves to eternal torment, and they

are boasting of this lawless deed!... This is how much malice dims the spiritual eye—the wretched man cannot see his own doom. Thus he sins doubly: he sins and boasts of his sin: "See, I showed him. Now he knows with whom he has trifled!..." Yes, he knows who you are, knows your hatred too, and that you brought harm to him, but do you know yourself, where and in what condition you are? Do you realize that you have harmed yourself more than him? It is his flesh that you have hurt, but it is your soul that you have doomed with your revenge. He, because of your slander, is judged and loathed by people, but you are judged by God Himself. Him you have subjected to temporary infamy and humiliation, but yourself—to eternal ones! Hear what the Psalmist has to say to you: *Why dost thou, O mighty man, boast of iniquity in thy mischief?* And note what he adds further: *Therefore may God destroy thee forever, may he pluck thee up and utterly remove thee from thy dwelling, and thy root from the land of the living* (Psalm 52:1,5). This is why St. Chrysostom says: "When we are filled with malice and insidiousness against others, then we are sharpening our sword against ourselves and are inflicting much graver wounds on ourselves than on the others."

Many, because of their spite, reach such madness and become so blinded that they prefer to destroy themselves than to give up revenge. "I will ruin my enemy," they say, "even if I die in the process!" What are you uttering in your rage, blind and wretched creature? You want to doom yourself if only that would also destroy your brother, for whom Christ, the Son of God, died? Come to your senses, remember who you are, and know whose spirit works in you! Is it not the spirit of the one who himself perished, destroyed our forefathers, and with them us, too? He always plants malice in order to destroy us. Christ wants to save both you and him (your brother); but you want to ruin both him and yourself. But look and see against whom you are rebelling and arming yourself. He says: *He that is not with Me is against Me* (Matt. 12:30). With your own death you seek the death of your neighbor, and that is why you are not with Christ, but against Him Who desires both your and your neighbor's salvation so much that He shed His blood for it. With your actions you show that you are of one mind with that evil spirit who seeks to bring death to you, your neighbor, and all other men.... But in the heat of your anger you are crying: "I myself will die, but I will ruin him also!..." Of course, you can destroy yourself if you desire that, but you cannot destroy your neighbor if he is living with the grace and help of the Most High. And is it possible that you do not realize what is that ruin which you so desire for both yourself and your neighbor? Put your hand in the fire, and you will find out partly what the ruin is. If you cannot endure this small fire, how will you endure the eternal fire which burns but does not shine, scorches but does not burn down, torments but does not kill? With such a fire the malicious will be heated to red if they do not repent, and they will be burned and tormented both on the outside and from the inside without end. But the man blinded by hatred does not see this and screams in his rage: "I may perish, but I will not let my neighbor be!..."

O spite, devil's daughter—spite, how you blind the poor man! He wants to doom himself if only his neighbor will die too. There cannot be a greater madness than seeking the ruin of your neighbor through your own perdition. Many of the malicious refrain from fish, milk, eggs, meat—things which God has not forbidden but has even allowed to be used with thanksgiving and prayer; and the same spiteful people want to devour God's people alive! Many do not eat anything on Wednesdays and Fridays, but they do not want to fast from their hatred even for a minute, even though God is threatening them with eternal torment. Such a great and terrible evil spite is! It captivates the heart and blinds the mind so fatally! It is the vice which is most characteristic of the devil who himself perished and now seeks to lead the rest to that doom.[1]

---

1. St. Tikhon of Zadonsk, *On True Christianity*, pp. 206, 208.

IV

Reconciliation

IT HAS NOW been sufficiently shown what a deadly vice strife is—the man who carries spite in his breast is rearing a poisonous snake in his bosom. You know, kind readers, from your own experience, how heavy your soul is when you have quarreled with someone. It is as if a mountain weighs you down; you cannot breathe lightly and freely. You feel like a captive and even worse than that, because for the captive the body is bound but the spirit is free. For you, the spirit is bound with the chains of satanic strife, and the body also feels weakened because of this. The man who quarrels with his neighbor is a slave of the devil. Are there any happy slaves? If the bird, confined in a cage is happy, then the wretched captives of sin can also be happy. No! No happiness can bloom among the weeds of sin, and even less among the thorns and thistles of hatred and strife. While you are feuding with your brother, peace cannot rise in your heart!

On the other hand, how light your soul feels when you are reconciled with your enemy! You want, like a bird freed from a cage, to fly up to the skies with joy. You rejoice more at a reconciliation than at the discovery of a treasure. Indeed, you have found something more precious than riches; you have found love, won over your enemy, and have turned him from a foe into a brother. Simple folk express it very well: "Strife is a work of the devil." This is why it brings such darkness into the soul, oppresses it, and torments it as if it were already in hell. The grace of God which brings peace and joy to the heart flees from the spiteful. If "strife is a work of the devil," reconciliation is the work of God. Peace is one of the most precious of God's gifts. With the arrival of reconciliation, darkness disappears from the souls of those who until then have been filled with spite; and the peace of God, the light of God, and the joy of God settle there. God's grace descends on the reconciled, and they feel as if they were in Paradise.

Here are two examples from life in Russia.

In a village there served a priest who was constantly quarreling with the church reader. The reader had not finished seminary and thus he could not become a priest, so his dream was at least to be made a deacon. Unfortunately, he could not count on the support of the priest whom he hated and with whom he rudely quarreled. Once during service the priest and the reader quarreled over something; the priest raised his voice, the reader did not yield and answered with insulting words. The priest was enraged and tried to hit the reader with the incense-burner. The latter threw several heavy books at the priest, until in the end they literally began fighting, to the great chagrin and temptation of the people. The rumor of the fight of the priest and the reader in God's temple spread all over the village, and the case was reported to the bishop in the city as well. This bishop was a very wise man. He called the priest and the reader to himself to question them and find out who was to blame. He called the priest first and asked him:

"Tell me how it all happened. Honestly confess the truth!"

"I, holy Bishop, was serving in the church," the scared priest began to justify himself, "and I told the reader to read more slowly, but he attacked me with insults, began to throw the church books at me, and even hit me with his fists. I grabbed the incense-burner to defend myself, but I did not do anything to him."

"So he is to blame?" asked the prelate.

"Yes, holy Bishop, he is to blame!"

"So he started the fight?"

"Yes, Bishop, he started the fight."

"Then you are a martyr," continued the prelate. "You poor man, how long you have put up with this spiteful reader, and you have never complained! This is what I have thought of to reward you with a compensation: tomorrow I will elevate you to the rank of archpriest. Do you hear, child, even tomorrow! Get ready!"

The priest was moved by the unexpected turn of the matter and said: "But, Bishop, I am not worthy to be an archpriest. I am guilty of the quarrels too, and, it seems, my guilt is greater than the reader's. I started the quarrels!"

"So, there is a conscience in you? Praise God, praise God!" rejoiced the prelate. "Then you fully deserve the rank of archpriest."

The priest, repenting, began to cry.

Then the bishop sent for the reader. The reader came in worried and saw that the priest was crying and that the prelate did not stand grim and stern, but was smiling in a fatherly way.

"What do you say? Who started the fight?" asked the prelate.

"It was not me, but the priest!" said the frightened reader to justify himself.

"The priest said the same, that he is to blame. That means that you are innocent. Because you endured innocently, like a martyr, the insults of the priest for such a long time, I have decided to ordain you as a deacon tomorrow! Are you ready?"

The reader expected a punishment, but now he was being offered the deaconship that he had dreamed of for so long! Yet his soul was so disturbed! He felt so unprepared because of his quarrel with the priest. Suddenly, he fell at the feet of the bishop and said through his tears: "Holy Bishop, I am not worthy to be a deacon. I am more to blame than the priest."

The bishop lifted him up from the ground and, embracing him, said: "It is today that you are most worthy, because you repent, just as the priest repented. That is why I will certainly make him an archpriest and you, a deacon. Make peace!"

The two recent enemies embraced and forgave each other with deep contrition. On the next day, during the Divine Service, the bishop rewarded both of them with clerical ranks and sent them to their village in peace.

They returned reconciled and joyful, to the wonder of the whole village. From that day they lived like true brothers and never quarreled again.

Here is another example—again from Russia.

The priest and the deacon in one church hated each other immensely and constantly quarreled. It must not surprise you, brothers and sisters, that the clergy too may quarrel sometimes. They defend the spiritual fortress—the Church—and so the devil attacks them most. The priest and the deacon lived in strife for a long time, and, in the end, their hostility reached such a level that they could not even stand to look at each other. Their life was poisoned. At last, the priest could not endure living in this way any longer and went to a hermitic saint for advice. He told the hermit everything: how he and the deacon fought over the smallest things; how their hatred grew with each day; how the deacon, even though he was of lower rank, did not honor the priest; how he, the priest, could not stand him any longer and had decided to leave the parish. "What is your advice?" asked the priest in the end.

The holy hermit gave him the best and the hardest prescription: "Hold your tongue and have patience! Endure forever, and God will help you to turn your enemy around and win him over." The priest decided to try this as a last resort.

When he went back, it happened that he had to perform a service with the deacon. During the rite, he asked the deacon gently: "Hand me the cross."

"Take it yourself!" answered the deacon crossly. "I am not your servant."

The priest, without saying a word, went and took the cross. The deacon was surprised that the usual abuse and insults did not follow. The next time when the two had to serve together, the deacon scolded the priest for some reason, but the latter meekly endured and put up with everything. This went on for quite a while.... The priest always endured quietly, until at last the deacon began to recover his senses and was ashamed of his behavior.

"How bad I am!" he thought. "I am a deacon, and I bully the priest. He is greater than I, but he does not scold me and puts up with me! I will go to him and ask for his forgiveness!"

How surprised and moved the patient priest was when he saw the deacon coming to him in his house, bowing down to the ground before him, and asking for forgiveness with tears in his eyes. They embraced and forgave; and as much as they hated each other before, they loved each other afterwards. Such are the marvelous fruits of mutual forgiveness!

Joseph and his brothers.
From the Slavonic Bible, St. Petersburg, 1904.

V

Knowledge and Practice

WE ALL KNOW this, but still we do not practice it. Knowledge will not save us by itself if we do not begin to fulfill God's will. Knowledge without practice will condemn us on the strength of the words of Christ: *And that servant which knew his lord's will, and prepared not himself, neither did according to his will, shall be beaten with many stripes... For unto whomsoever much is given, of him shall be much required: and to whom men have committed much, of him they will ask the more* (Luke 12:47-48).

I had an interesting case in my own life which I would like to share with you, dear readers. Once a friend of mine came to me and said: "I am very hurt. My soul is deeply wounded by the insults which my relatives hurled at me. I cannot forgive them. I will demand my right; I will bring them to court." After hearing him out I tried to calm him down and, to change his mind, reminded him how much the righteous of God have been insulted and slandered; how they, even though they suffered without guilt, endured everything bravely; that we should endure even more so, because our souls are filled with sins, and that if we forgive, God will forgive us also, etc., etc. I told him that we gain great benefit from the endurance of unjust insults,

89

and in support of this, I read to him the following edifying example from the *Handbook for Spiritual Life*:

In a monastery close to Alexandria, there lived an elder who was very cross.... A young monk, hearing about him, made a vow before God, saying: "Lord, for the expiation of all the sins which I have committed, I will go to this elder and live with him, serve him as a slave, and will endure everything patiently." And so he did. He went to the elder and settled down to live there with him. The elder treated him like a dog and sneered at him every day. After six years of living together, a dreadful angel appeared to the young monk in a dream holding a long scroll in his hands. The angel told him that half of the sins recorded on the scroll had been erased by God and that he should take care of the rest.

Not far away from this cross elder lived another, more righteous ascetic. He could hear how the other elder mistreated the brother and how the latter asked for forgiveness, but the elder did not give it to him. When he happened to meet the young monk, the righteous elder always asked him: "How are you, child? How did the day go? Did we win something? Did we blot something out from the list?" The brother, knowing that the elder was a godly man, did not hide his secrets from him, but answered: "Yes, Father, today, we struggled a little." When he spent the day in peace, when he was not scolded, nor beaten, nor driven away, then in the evening he went crying to the godly elder and said to him through tears: "Alas, Father, today's day was fruitless: we did not gain anything; we spent the whole day in peace...."

When another six years passed, the brother passed away. Then the godly elder said that he had seen this brother standing before God among the martyrs and praying to God for his elder: "Lord, as You pardoned me through him, so pardon him for

Your goodness' sake and for the sake of me, Your slave." When forty days passed, the brother took to himself in the place of rest his repentant elder....[1]

When I read this book to my friend, I waited to see how he would react. He was moved to tears and said: "Indeed, how great the Holy Fathers were! What patience they had!" I told him: "Here, my dear, is a way for salvation for you, too: forgive the people who have hurt you, and God will forgive you!" Suddenly, he, as if something stung him, remembered his trouble and cried: "I, to forgive? I cannot! They hurt my honor terribly. I will demand my right! I will bring them to court." With these words he left....

Beloved readers, do we not all act in the same way as this friend of mine? We are moved to tears when we read in our warm and cozy rooms about the feats of the great righteous ones of God. We cry tenderly when we see their patience. Our souls melt when we listen to nice sermons about them; but when in our life we meet our personal enemy or the one with whom we quarreled yesterday, we turn our backs on him and cannot forgive him. Of what use is our knowledge of how we should act or of how the saints have acted in such cases if we do not do as they have done?

---

1. *Handbook for Spiritual Life*, p. 66.

Forgiveness, by Rembrandt, 1636.

VI

The Man Who Forgives Will Be Forgiven

GOD HAS COMMANDED us to put an end to our quarrels and strife and to forgive insults not because He needs these things, but because they are beneficial to us. Whoever forgives his neighbor's sins will himself receive pardon from God according to the promise of the Savior, and how many sins we have before God! What fear should come over us when we remember that we will have to answer for all of them at the Day of Judgment! To our great shame, all our dark deeds will be revealed to the universe at the terrible Judgment of God. Then we will not be able to expiate them in any way. However, now the Savior is offering us an easy way to erase all our sins: *"Forgive, and ye shall be forgiven"* (Luke 6:37). Forgive from your heart the small sins of your brother against you, and you will receive pardon for all your countless sins before God! Is there anything better and more favorable than this? If love for God and His holy commandments cannot make us forgive, then let us forgive for our own interest at least! But alas, often not only the high motives of disinterested virtue, but even the insistent calls of our own interest are not able to induce us to forgive. Our spitefulness has blinded us so that it has made us our own greatest enemy. In strife we are going against God with open eyes; we aim the blade of our spite at our own heart; we poison our health; and we ourselves seek eternal doom for our soul. Is there anything more foolish than this?

How good it is to forgive! The soul feels so light and pleasant afterwards! One feels such a tenderness after having forgiven that he is ready to embrace the whole world, to start loving everyone and to forgive everything. At that, it is not difficult to forgive; a little courage of the soul and some mercy of the heart are all that is required for the purpose. Numb your pride, and it will be easy to forgive your neighbor! Drive away the hatred from your heart, and you will win the love of your brother! Defeat spite, that enemy of yours, in your soul, and you will make a friend out of your enemy. When you overcome in this way the enemy within you, you will disarm the enemy without as well. It is not required of you to give anything to the person with whom you have quarreled. Only forgive him from your heart! For such forgiveness, God will not only forgive your own innumerable sins, but He will also present you with the most precious of all treasures—the Kingdom of Heaven, the eternal joy of Paradise!

Happy is he who quickly drives spite out of his heart. He does not trouble his soul here, and in heaven he will abide forever among the angels. Let us too, beloved, as we know this, be always ready to be reconciled to our enemies. Let us not excuse ourselves with the fact that the other person does not want to be reconciled to us. Even if he does not want to forgive us, what is preventing us from forgiving him? If he wants to commit spiritual suicide through strife, is it wise for us to inflict the same misfortune upon ourselves?

How often in life one hears similar excuses: "How can I forgive him when he does not come to me? He is lesser than I; let him be the first to extend his hand for reconciliation! He offended me, that is why he must apologize first! I do not have anything against him, but if he does not want to make peace, I do not want to either. Who—I—to go first and ask for forgiveness?! Why should I be humiliated before him? What is he? I have dignity, too," etc. Have we ourselves not said the preceding words before one time or another? We probably have, but these words only accuse; they do not excuse their authors. Jesus Christ has never said that we should forgive only when our opponents come to ask our pardon. He has never determined that the lesser one should ask first for forgiveness. Everyone is to forgive his personal enemy each time and for everything that has hurt his pride. If the one who started the quarrel comes to his senses first and humbly asks his opponent for forgiveness, he will erase the guilt of his soul; and if the innocent remains irreconcilable in his pride, he will become even guiltier than the one who started the fight. It is good for the younger party to make the first step toward reconciliation, but if he does not have the sense to do so, nothing prevents the older or higher in rank to humble himself first. A moving example of such humility is found in the life of St. John the Merciful, the Patriarch of Alexandria. Once, St. John was serving the Divine Liturgy when he suddenly remembered that one of his subordinates from the lower clergy was angry with him for something. Then St. John, the Patriarch, left the holy throne, called the lower clergyman to himself, and fell at his feet asking him for forgiveness. The clergyman was disturbed and ashamed by the great humility of the Patriarch and himself fell at the Saint's feet and cried with tears: "Forgive me, Father." In this way, St. John showed by example that even those with higher status can ask first for forgiveness and that the humility of the greater affects their subordinates very powerfully.

The Holy Fathers teach us that the one who forgives always wins. Whatever the occasion may be, if you forgive, you immediately cleanse your soul and become fit for Paradise. If you have forgiven those who have plotted to murder you, you have become equal to the martyrs. If you have forgiven an insult, you have gained peace and have won the Kingdom of Heaven. If you have generously overlooked the rumors and slanders against you, you have dulled the sting of your foe. If you have returned good for evil, you have shamed your enemy. If you have swallowed a sarcastic insult to your honor, you have become worthy of heavenly honors. If, being of higher rank in life, you have asked the pardon of a lesser man, you have not only *not* disgraced yourself, but you have furthered your spiritual maturity. If you were not to blame but asked the offender to forgive you, you have thus helped his soul to be delivered from the hell of hatred and have covered many of your own sins, too. If you have abased your pride, you have exalted your humility.

Let us suppose that you are quarreling with your neighbors because they have taken and misused money belonging to you, and they do not want to return it. What should you do to respond in a Christian way? Let us discuss this case thoroughly, since it is very often that quarrels and even bloody fights occur between contemporary Christians over money, land, and inheritances. The vice of avarice makes us feel deeply hurt when someone has misappropriated money of ours but denies that it is ours and refuses to return it. We are ready to slander and revile such a man before all, to call him a thief, a bandit, and even to take him to court. Thus, on the occasion of his sin, we too begin to sin, and this is not right. He is headed to hell, and we are in a hurry to catch up with him, so that we will not be left out of the eternal fire.

What should we do so as not to sin? Jesus Christ says that we should forgive! Of course, we could gently ask him to pay the sum back. If our debtor realizes that it is a sin to steal other people's money and returns it to us, it will be good both for him and for us. But if he does not do so, we should leave everything to God and forgive. God has the ways and the power to reimburse us. We should have only one priority in mind—to shun sin! It is better to let ourselves be cheated than to take someone to court (cf. I Cor. 6:7)!

It is true that in this way we will lose something very precious to the body, but at the same time we will gain something even more precious for the soul: we will show that we esteem love for our neighbor more than money, and we will cut off the advance of hate into our soul! It is to teach us precisely this that Jesus Christ has left us the command: *If any man will sue thee at the law, and take away thy coat, let him have thy cloak also* (Matt. 5:40). This is what the righteous of God have done in the past. Here is an example: thieves attacked the poor cell of a desert-dweller in his absence. When the hermit returned, he saw the thieves carrying out his books and clothes. Then he, without getting angry, joined them and helped them to carry off his possessions....

The robber steals our property, but God sees everything. If we forgive, He will recompense us a hundredfold in heaven and will count the stolen property as alms given away. Then our enemy will be turned against his will into our benefactor, and with his help we will be saved more easily. If we endure and forgive our robbers we may seem foolish in the eyes of the world, but in the eyes of God we will be wise. Our souls will derive a great benefit from our forgiveness and long-suffering. We will not view then that which was stolen from us as lost, and it will be much easier for us to endure the other misfortunes in this life.

I will give you evidence from the writings of the Holy Fathers so that you will be convinced that these are not empty words but teachings of the Holy Church. This is what St. John Chrysostom has to say concerning the matter: "Someone has deprived you of money! If you endure its loss bravely, you will receive the same reward as if you had given it to the poor. Actually, the man who gives money to the poor and the man who for God's sake forgives the man who robbed him and does not even say a bad word to him are doing the same thing"[1] A wonderful confirmation of this thought is found in the life of the Reverend Areta of the Kiev Caves.[2] This is what is told about him:

Fr. Areta was living in the monastery of Kiev Caves. He had one great weakness: he was a miser. He secretly accumulated a lot of money in his cell, and he neither gave of it to others nor spent it for his own needs. One night thieves stole all of his riches. He was so grieved that he almost destroyed himself. His heart was filled with malice, and he began to attack and torment the innocent people around him. The brothers advised him to calm down, but he would not listen and became more and more hateful of everyone.

After some time, he fell seriously ill and was close to death. All the while, though, he did not stop grumbling and reviling. However, God brought him to his senses in a miraculous way. Once, Fr. Areta was lying in a deadly stupor when suddenly he began crying before all: "Lord, have mercy! Lord, forgive me! Lord, I have sinned! It is Yours, I do not grieve for it!" He immediately got up from his bed and explained to the gathered monks the cause of his cry: "I saw," he said, "that angels and a crowd of demons came to me and began arguing about my soul. The demons were saying: 'He did not give thanks to God for

---

1. *Works,* XII, p. 611.
2. *Lives of the Saints,* October 24.

the theft but reviled Him. That is why he is ours and will be delivered into our hands!' But the angels said to me: 'Wretched man, if you had thanked God for the theft of your treasure, it would have been counted as alms, as was Job's. The giving of alms is a great deed before God because through it a man reveals his good will. If a man has been robbed and endures with thanksgiving, that resistance to the devil's temptation is counted for good will; for the devil does those things to make the man blaspheme, but a grateful person turns everything over to God, and that is equal to the giving of alms.' When the angels said that, I cried: 'Lord, forgive me! Lord, I have sinned! It is yours, I do not grieve for it!' The demons disappeared immediately, and the angels rejoiced, and after accepting the lost treasure instead of alms, they left."

When the brothers heard this, they praised God Who seeks to turn even the worst to the benefit of man. After this occurrence, Fr. Areta changed and corrected his life so much that he became one of the great Kiev Caves Saints.

The Holy Fathers always endured with thanksgiving all misfortunes in their lives. They knew that the man who endures patiently every suffering, unjust insult, or intentional harm to their personal interests is saving his soul with his patience. By losing the temporal, he gains the eternal. This is why they never got angry with other people nor quarreled with their enemies. Patience and long-suffering toward their personal enemies were important virtues in the development of their holy personal life. How right the Holy Fathers were! Do you realize this, dear reader? If you do, it is good for your soul, but if, remembering about your enemies and debtors, you shake your head with disapproval because you cannot imagine how you could forgive the villain who has stolen and used your money, nor how you could be reconciled with the hag who has insulted you so viciously, then you are not on the right road—for it is exactly those personal and hateful enemies that we are commanded to forgive. If you are still tormented by malevolent moods, you have not yet tasted the sweetness of forgiving; your fleshly interests still stand higher than your spiritual ones. You, entangled in the nets of earthly things, cannot fly up to the horizons of the spirit where Jesus Christ is preparing great bliss for His followers. If, however, you feel that the Holy Fathers advise us correctly, even though they neglect our material and temporal interests somewhat by teaching us to forgive our enemies, if you are moved and gladdened at the reading of these lines, however foolish they may seem to the world, happy are you—for you have found the path that leads to the Kingdom of Heaven.

VII

Endurance and Salvation

So FAR the discussion has dealt mostly with two possible relationships between people—strife and mutual reconciliation. The third relationship which is possible between the quarrelers—that in which one is ready to forgive, but the other is irreconcilable—was mentioned too, especially in the last chapter. Here, we will complete and clarify the treatment of that third relationship.

In the spirit of Christ's teachings, the man who is wiser and more mature spiritually should forgive generously in his heart, even though the other does not want to even hear about making peace. The good Christian should endure to the end with patience the troubles which his enemy brings him. *But he that shall endure unto the end, the same shall be saved* (Matt. 24:13), the Savior teaches us, or, in short, endurance saves. Our Lord Jesus Christ has given us a moving example of endurance and forgiveness when He suffered without complaining on Golgotha and prayed from the cross for His cruel enemies: *Father, forgive them, for they know not what they do* (Luke 23:34). St. Stephen the Archdeacon acted in the same way by praying for his murderers while they were stoning him: *Lord, lay not this sin to their charge* (Acts 7:60). All Holy Fathers, all holy martyrs, all revered and saints have acted in the very same way. All of them found the shortest way to Paradise through endurance and forgiveness. This is why they have left us the legacy to act like them. If we quarrel, let us be reconciled quickly! If we make peace with our enemy, our success is double: we have snatched both ourselves and him from the claws of the evil one. If we do not succeed in persuading our enemy to be reconciled, we should not continue in our spitefulness towards him, we should not hate him as he hates us so that the loss will not be doubled and our soul perish together with his. In such cases, the wisest thing we can do is to forgive him, so that if he perishes at least we will not be devoured by the devil. If we forgive him and put up with him our salvation is certain, because endurance is no small feat. According to the Holy Fathers, endurance equals martyrdom. This is why the long-suffering and forgiving, even though they may have sinned much in the past, will be crowned with imperishable crowns like the holy martyrs. To inspire us to long-suffering and endurance, the Holy Fathers teach us that those who flatter us are our enemies and those that insult us are our benefactors. St. John Chrysostom has some wonderful thoughts on this subject. Let us listen to him:

> When the enemy derides you for some sin which you see in yourself, and you, hearing this, do not answer him with insults but begin to sigh and to entreat God, you will smooth over your sin. Lest you think that I am merely consoling you with empty words, I will call on the testimony of Holy Scripture. There were a Pharisee and a Publican. The latter had reached the vilest depths of sin, and the former jealously guarded his righteousness. Once, both of them went to the temple to pray. The Pharisee stood and said: *God, I thank Thee, that I am not as other men are, extortioners, unjust, adulterers, or even as this*

The Publican and the Pharisee, from the original
Bulgarian text of *Strife & Reconciliation*.

publican, (Luke 18:11). And the Publican, standing on
the side, did not answer with insults, and did not say any
sinful words like those that we hurl at each other every
day, but sighed bitterly and *smote upon his breast, saying,
God, be merciful to me a sinner* (Luke 18:13), and went
away justified. Do you see how quickly he was justified?
He got soiled, and he washed away the spot; he realized
his sins and was released from them; the accusation of sin
turned into a loosening of sin, and the enemy became a
benefactor against his own will. Is there anything more
gracious than this? Is there any other, easier way of
breaking free from sin? Otherwise, how long the Publican
would have labored, fasted, kept vigil, lain on the ground,

given away his property to the poor, and sat in ashes in order to erase his sins. Now, without doing any of these things, he was freed from all sin and disgrace with just a word. The slander of the man who had obviously insulted him brought him the crown of righteousness without long-lasting efforts and labors.[1]

Such are the fruits of true Christian endurance and long-suffering. The man who is not quick to anger and knows how to endure is helping his own salvation. The man who does not immediately take offense, but waits meekly, is humble. The humble one always seeks the blame for everything that befalls him in himself and never in others. Thus, having realized that he himself is to blame for the insults which are hurled at him, he is angry with himself and not with others. He unites with those that attack him, and in this way, in alliance with his enemies, he easily and quickly drives away the real enemy of his soul—sin. The man who quarrels with his attackers takes the side of his own sin, defends it, and thus strengthens it in his soul. Such a man is proud, and it is difficult for him to be saved. St. John Chrysostom asks the offended:

Why do you refuse to be reconciled to your enemy? He is speaking ill of you, calling you a fornicator? So what? If he is speaking the truth, correct yourself, if not—laugh at it!... And even better, not only laugh but rejoice ... according to the Word of God: *Blessed are ye, when men shall hate you, and when they shall separate you from their company, and shall reproach you, and cast out your name as evil, for the Son of Man's sake. Rejoice ye in that day and leap for joy: For, behold, your reward is great in heaven*

---

1. *Works*, XII, p. 514.

(Luke 6:22-23). And if he has spoken the truth, and you ... condemn your transgressions, you will receive a reward.... Often the enemies with their just rebuke accomplish that which your friends cannot with their praises and pleasant words.[2]

If we, beloved Christian readers, are patient with our enemies and seek the blame for their unkind attitude towards us in ourselves, we will be saved.

A young and spiritually immature monk went to live in a certain monastery. He thought that there he would find paradisiacal manners and that everyone would love and respect him as a most dear brother. What was his disappointment when after a while he noticed that eight of the brothers loved him and two did not! He could not put up with the dislike of these two, so he left that monastery and went to search for another where everyone would like him. In the second monastery, all brothers welcomed him kindly and treated him very well in the beginning. However, that did not last very long. Soon the likes and dislikes toward the newcomer surfaced, and, unfortunately, this time only four loved him and four others hated him and were worse than those in the first monastery: they annoyed him, judged him, sneered at him, and did not miss an occasion to hurt him. The unhappy monk could not put up with that, so he left this monastery, too. In the third monastery where he settled, he quickly found out that almost nobody liked him. His reputation for being quarrelsome and lacking perseverance preceded him to this monastery, and the brothers there met him with distrust. The young monk, realizing that he had come from bad to worse, began wondering if it was not his fault that he

---

2. *Works,* XII, p. 613.

could not win the love of the others and decided to remain in this last monastery amid the cold and hostile attitudes of the brothers until he could win their love with God's help. When he appraised his own behavior, he found that he was to blame for his quarrels with the brothers because he did not endure their teasing with patience. A fortunate thought occurred to him, and he wrote on a piece of paper: "I will endure everything for Jesus Christ's sake" and put it in his belt. Every time when someone insulted him or sneered at him, he took the piece of paper out of his belt, read it, remembered the promise of endurance which he had made to God, and calmed down. Some of the brothers wondered at his patience and began to love him. Others, in their malice, said: "He is doing some kind of magic to calm himself. Whenever we annoy him, he takes a piece of paper out of his belt, and when he looks at it, his anger passes away. This business is not good. He must be a magician...." With such suspicions in their hearts the spiteful monks went to the abbot and slandered the young brother before him. The abbot investigated the matter, found out the innocence of the brother, and for his justification and as a lesson to all, he summoned all monks to himself. When the accusations against the young brother were repeated, the abbot ordered him to show the piece of paper before everyone. The young monk obeyed, took out the paper, and read the writing: "I will endure everything for Jesus Christ's sake." Then the accusers were ashamed and silenced, and the brother, acquitted and praised, lived peacefully with the respect and love of the monks.

In the same way, if we endure everything for Jesus Christ's sake, we will be saved. When we quarrel and fight, we always consider ourselves right and the others guilty. This is a result of our pride, and pride is the greatest obstacle to the peace of our soul. When no one bothers us, we are calm and consider ourselves very good. But when someone offends us, we get insulted and enraged and think that the other person is the cause of our anger. No, he is not to blame for it! The real cause is in the passions that are dormant in us. They have dozed quietly while they were not irritated, but at the first occasion they show their sting. The man who has insulted us is not to blame that we are so proud, touchy, and sensitive that we cannot endure even the least offense. The fact that the offender can even bring benefit to a meek and humble soul, and that he becomes a cause of sin only for the proud one, testifies very clearly that the offender cannot be considered guilty for our spitefulness and strife. He only provides an occasion for the feelings that are already hidden in our soul to gush forth. If a man breaks moldy bread which has grown musty inside but has retained its good outward look, is he to blame for the mold on the bread? With our hidden passions we resemble whitewashed tombs: wonderful on the outside and filled with stench on the inside. According to the instructions of the Holy Fathers, if we want to be corrected, we should blame ourselves and not get angry at others. Instead of getting angry at the brother who has become the occasion for our passions to explode, we should rather thank him for helping us to know ourselves.

Happy is he who has learned that he himself is to blame for his own sins. This realization will lead him to repentance; the repentance—to humility; the humility—to endurance; and the endurance—to salvation.

A peaceful scene from 19th-century Russia. V. D. Polenov, 1878.

VIII

Conclusion

As WE CONCLUDE the question of strife and reconciliation, we should repeat the three possible relationships among people. We saw that people cannot live in perfect peace, since sin is present among them. Henceforth, they are either hostile to one another to the grave, which is the most terrible condition for a soul; or they forgive each other; or if one of them cannot be reconciled, the other endures and forgives him.

In which of these three situations are we to be found, dear Christians? If we forgive, all is well; but if we do not, we are most wretched, because we ourselves defy God not to forgive us. In the Lord's prayer we call to God to treat us in the same way that we treat our neighbors: *and forgive our debts as we forgive our debtors.* How will God forgive us when we do not forgive?

In the life of St. Basil the New it is said that the last trial with which the souls passing to the other world are tested is the trial of mercifulness. This is not so by accident, but in accordance with God's law. If you have observed and fulfilled all commandments and avoided all sins, but you have remained irreconcilable and bitter towards your personal enemy, you will not enter the Kingdom of Heaven. Only the merciful will be shown mercy. The man who has been lenient towards others will enjoy God's lenience toward his own weaknesses. The spiteful will remain unforgiven. St. Tikhon of Zadonsk says clearly: "The doors of God's mercy open before the thieves, murderers, fornicators, publicans, and all other sinners, but they close before the spiteful."[1] God is very merciful and long-suffering. If we want to go to Him, we must come to resemble Him at least partially: we must become merciful and lenient toward our neighbors, and we must endure their weaknesses with great patience.

God says: *I will have mercy and not sacrifice* (cf. Hosea 6:6; Matt. 9:13). Mercy in our heart, love for our neighbors, and not great sacrifices which often serve as food to our pride and vanity! Mercy and not sacrifice! Humility and reconciliation among us and not pride and discord!

On every holy day we go to church for Divine Liturgy. There we want to offer God our small sacrifice: to light a candle, to drop our alms in the box for the poor, to pray to the Savior. But on the way to church we meet our neighbor with whom we have quarreled yesterday, and we pass by him and turn our face away from him with disgust. Do we consider that God too will turn away His face from us? Until we are reconciled—or, if the other one does not want to be reconciled, at least until we forgive—God will not accept either our sacrifice or our prayer. If we forgive our neighbors their transgressions from our heart, then and only then will God forgive us, and we will be able to pray boldly: *And forgive us our debts as we forgive our debtors,* because He Himself has said: *Forgive, and ye shall be forgiven* (Luke 6:37).

Amen.

---

1. *Works,* p. 414.

Index

INDEX

L

Last Judgment, 18, 70, 93
Lausiac History, The, 36
Lives of the Saints, The, 74 n., 77 n.,
   98 n.
Lukia, St., 25 ill.

M

Macarius of Alexandria, St., 56-57,
   59
Macarius the Great, St., 51
Moscow, 40
Moses, Prophet, 41
Mother of God, Most Holy
   Joy of All Who Sorrow Icon, 2
   ill.

N

Nicephorus of Antioch, 74-77
Nile River, 37
Novgorod, 72

O

On True Christianity, 82 n.
Orthodoxy and Ecumenism, 8
Our Hope, 8
Our Love, 8

P

Palladius, Bishop, 36
Paradise, 18-21, 34, 52, 54, 59, 70,
   94, 96, 102
Paul, Apostle, 4, 22, 24, 26, 34, 46
   ill., 47, 51, 77
Peaceful Scene, A, 108 ill.
Peter, Apostle, 4, 40
Pharisee, the, 102, 103 ill.
Poemen the Long-suffering, St., 56
Polenov, V. D., 108
Publican, the, 102, 103 ill.

R

Russia, 10, 16, 40, 72, 84, 86, 108
Russky Palomnik, 78 ill.

S

Saint Helen Island, 40
Saint Petersburg, 88
Sanhedrin, the, 23
Sapricius, Priest of Antioch, 74-77
Seraphim (Aleksiev), Archiman-
   drite, 6 ill., 7-8
Seraphim of Sarov, St., 7 n., 20, 20
   n., 26, 28
Seraphim (Sobolev), Archbishop, 7,
   7 n.
Sofia, Bulgaria, 8
stavroclasm, 7 n.
Stephen, Protomartyr, 101
Supplicatory Prayer, 41 ill.
Switzerland, 7
Sypanov Trinity Monastery, 10

T

Theophan the Recluse, St., 60
Tikhon of Zadonsk, St., 68, 78 ill.,
   79, 82 n., 110
Titus, Hieromonk of Kiev Caves,
   73-74

U

Unconsolable Sorrow, 16 ill.

W

War, 72 ill.
Works of St. John Chrysostom, 98 n.,
   104 n., 105 n.
Works of St. Tikhon of Zadonsk, 68
   n., 110 n.